# *The* ARCHITECTURAL JEWELS *of* ROCHESTER

### NEW HAMPSHIRE

*A History* of the *Built Environment*

## MICHAEL BEHRENDT

*Kitty,*
*welcome to the HDC. You will be a terrific addition. Enjoy.*

Charleston · London

THE
History
PRESS

Published by The History Press
Charleston, SC 29403
www.historypress.net

First published 2009

*Front cover, bottom*: Photograph of mural by Eve Edelstein.

Manufactured in the United States

ISBN 978.1.59629.796.8

Library of Congress Cataloging-in-Publication Data

Behrendt, Michael (Michael David), 1955-
The architectural jewels of Rochester : a history of the built environment / Michael
Behrendt.
p. cm.
Includes bibliographical references.
ISBN 978-1-59629-796-8
1. Architecture--New Hampshire--Rochester. 2. Rochester (N.H.)--Buildings,
structures, etc. I. Title.
NA735.R58B44 2009
720.9742'5--dc22
2009036412

*This book is dedicated to Yvette Behrendt,*
*my wise, supportive and ever-enthusiastic mother.*
*If Yvette were a building, she would be a Queen Anne.*

*Men do not love Rome because she is beautiful;*
*Rome is beautiful because men have loved her.*
*—Leopold Kohr*

# Contents

# CONTENTS

# Preface

*There was a time in our past when one could walk down any street and be surrounded by harmonious buildings…The old buildings smiled, while our new buildings are faceless. The old buildings sang, while the buildings of our age have no music in them.*
—*Jonathan Hale,* The Old Way of Seeing

I set out writing this book to laud the heritage of Rochester, New Hampshire, where I work as the chief planner. While this community's legacy is worthy of praise, I soon realized that I had a larger purpose.

The human habitat is in tatters. We have come to accept a world with unsightly buildings and a diminished public realm as our inevitable fate. We do not believe it can be otherwise because, as a nation, we have forgotten what the face of beauty in the built environment looks like. Yet, in spite of the ravages of modern society, we have an extraordinary patrimony all around to help us relearn.

Good design matters. Victor Hugo said, "The beautiful is as useful as the useful…and perhaps more so." The character of our surroundings affects us profoundly, in how we relate to our fellow citizens, in the functioning of the economy, in our physical health and, truly, in our level of happiness.

To those readers who are not residents of Rochester, New Hampshire, I hope that this book inspires you to discover and celebrate the untold gems in your own community. I use Rochester as a springboard, but the bulk of the architectural styles and building types shown here are present everywhere.

# The Built Environment

Architecture is the heart of the human habitat, but there is more. The built environment, or "architecture" in a wider sense, encompasses everything that you see as you explore a city, town or village, including, among other things, buildings, bridges, stone walls, streets, street trees and stormwater culverts. This book explores a broad array of elements, but, I promise, there is no discussion of culverts.

# The Larger Setting

The protection of distinguished individual sites is important, but that is not sufficient. We admire the rich detailing of a cast-iron commercial storefront and the grandeur of a county courthouse, but if they are bounded by parking lots and dull one-story structures, then our experience is compromised. A harmonious ensemble of buildings equals a sum far greater than its parts. Human beings savor immersion in great places, where an embracing fabric fully engages us. This is why we love walking on Market Street in Portsmouth, New Hampshire; State Street in Newburyport, Massachusetts; or King Street in Alexandria, Virginia.

# New Urbanism

Preserving the historic context is essential, but why should we assume that we are not capable of creating another Portsmouth, Newburyport or Alexandria? As much joy as we derive from these destinations, it would be disheartening to believe that no more wonderful places will ever be built.

There is a movement today known as New Urbanism, composed of architects, planners, developers, engineers and interested citizens who are creating communities that merit our affection. The new urbanists have distilled the principles that underlie the appeal of the old places, and they are applying those standards to new projects across the country, albeit with a keen awareness of contemporary constraints.

New urbanists foster urbanity (or, more precisely, "urbanism") by establishing compact development patterns, mixing uses in a felicitous manner, designing streets for pedestrians as well as vehicles and promoting excellence in architecture. I discuss its concepts throughout the book.

# Rochester

All of the structures depicted here are located in one place, an unpretentious, old mill town near the seacoast of New Hampshire. There is a surprising abundance of outstanding architecture and plenty of local color in Rochester. The majority of properties presented are in private ownership, so please be considerate if you happen to drive (or, better yet, walk!) by them.

To the residents of Rochester, New Hampshire, I hope this small volume contributes to your appreciation of what a special community you live in.

I grew up in Rochester, New York (the other Rochester). May all of my old friends there buy this book, mistakenly thinking that it is about them.

# Introduction

*Rochester has hundreds of historic, architecturally significant, and beautiful buildings. It is easy to miss them. We are diverted as we race down the highway; myriad structures have been altered, often obscuring their noteworthy features; and all too many are now surrounded by incompatible development which distracts from their pedigree. Nonetheless, slow down, look around, look up. Check out the fancy cornices on North Main Street, admire the brickwork on our few remaining mill structures, and impress your friends by pointing out lintels, quoins, and lozenges.*
*—Opening paragraph in the inaugural article of the "Architectural Jewels" series in the* Rochester Times, *November 28, 2002*

This book is based on a twenty-eight-part newspaper series entitled "Rochester Has Many Architectural Jewels" that appeared biweekly in the *Rochester Times*. The series ran from Thanksgiving Day 2002 to Thanksgiving Day 2003.

I came to love architecture during a trip to Europe with my family during my sophomore year in high school. My parents treated my sister Gail and me to three fabulous weeks in London, Paris, Rome, Vienna and Madrid. My mother thought I was destined to wear a frock because she could not extricate me from the Gothic cathedrals.

After college I worked at The Architects Collaborative in Cambridge, Massachusetts, while attending the Boston Architectural Center at night. I gleaned much about the history of architecture but soon realized, in the course of ruthless critiques, that I had entirely no talent for drawing or design. Voila! A city planner was born.

# Newspaper Articles

I left my last planning job in Beaufort, South Carolina, fourteen years ago to assume my current position with the City of Rochester. On my first day here, I toured two manufacturing facilities with Mayor Harvey Bernier, a very humorous fellow. I figured, if the mayor is the funniest guy in town, Rochester must be all right.

The Rochester City Council appointed a task force to explore creating an ordinance to protect historic structures. The committee concluded that a historic district should be established, and in order to demonstrate its merits, I gave a slide show of significant properties to the council.

Afterward, John Nolan, the editor of the *Rochester Times*, suggested that I write a few articles for the newspaper, illustrating some of the buildings from the show. John and I thought we could put together three or four pieces. I never imagined that there would be twenty-eight articles when the series finished a year later. This is testimony to the extraordinary collection of architecture here. Who would think that this small, weathered city would have such a legacy!

# About Rochester

Rochester was named in honor of Jack Benny's chauffeur, Rochester van Jones…no, not really. We were, of course, named for Rochester, England (actually for the Earl of Rochester, an associate of the colonial governor). Rochester, England, located in the southeast corner of the country, is renowned for its cathedral and castle and an epic siege that occurred in 1215 (the same year the Magna Carta was signed).

There are about thirty thousand residents in Rochester, New Hampshire (and in Rochester, England). Our city is large enough to support a wide range of activities and businesses, yet it has an emphatic neighborly quality. Sir Ebenezer Howard, surely the only dude named Ebenezer ever to be knighted, a utopian nineteenth-century English city planner, argued that the ideal form of development was a network of self-contained "garden cities" surrounded by forests and farmland. He suggested that a population of thirty thousand residents divided into six wards (which we have, along with two intrepid council members from each) would lead to healthy and harmonious living for its citizens (Rochester, again).

Like Rome, Rochester was built on seven hills. Okay, I am the first person to ever make this claim and I admit to taking liberties in choosing which hills to count (our newfound backdrop of the White Mountains, shown on the cover of this book, notwithstanding). Nevertheless, Rochester is a gracious city with a noble patrimony, which will become evident as you read on.

The cover shows a mural of the greater downtown from the vantage point of Rochester Hill. It was painted in 1978 by John Woodsum Hatch and is an artistic interpretation of the city rather than a literal rendering. Profile Bank commissioned the painting and later donated it to Frisbie Hospital, where it now hangs in the cafeteria. Once you have read the book, see if you can find the following sites in the picture: the Congregational church, the Methodist church, the Hayes Block, the Elm Block, the Parson Main Statue, the St. Charles Home, Wyandotte Falls, the lower dam, the upper dam, the Emily Cross House, the library, Spaulding High School and Waldo.

# Organization of This Book

There are three parts in this book. Part I showcases architectural styles, Part II, building types and Part III, architectural elements. Each chapter provides background on the subject, including related topics (with a few ever so slight digressions), and then discusses a few specific properties in Rochester.

There is a photograph of each property. Unless otherwise noted, all images were taken by me. Each image is labeled with a caption that matches the heading for the corresponding text. The captions and headings identify the street where the property is located.

Architectural terms that the average person would not know are italicized and defined in the glossary. Some terms are also defined in the text, immediately following the use of the term. ***Please be sure to consult the glossary of architectural terms at the end when you encounter new terms***.* There are many more terms clustered in the early chapters, so you won't need to continually flip to the back of the book for long. Hang in there!

# *Part 1*

# ARCHITECTURAL STYLES

# THE GEORGIAN AND
# FEDERAL STYLES

*Show me the architecture of a people and I will tell you the story of their character, civilization, and refinement.*
*—anonymous*

Portsmouth and Dover, New Hampshire, were settled in 1623, three years after the Pilgrims landed at Plymouth, Massachusetts, and seven years prior to the Puritans' arrival in Boston. Due to conflicts with the Native American population, another one hundred years passed before newcomers ventured farther inland to establish themselves in Rochester in 1728.

## First Period

The original settlement of New England, from 1620 to the early 1700s, is known as the "First Period." There are about seventy surviving houses from this era in our region, primarily in Massachusetts and Connecticut. There are none in Rochester.

First Period houses were generally two floors with a one-story section added at the rear, resulting in the familiar *saltbox* shape. *Don't forget to consult the glossary at the end for italicized words.* They were built of heavy oak post and beam timbers and clad in unpainted wood clapboards or shingles. The steep roof kept the snow off, and a large central chimney warmed the family. Thick doors and small windows with leaded panes offered some protection from Native American attacks. These houses look as though they had been transplanted from the medieval era.

# Georgian Architecture

The Georgian style of architecture was named for Britain's Kings George I, II and III, who reigned consecutively through the eighteenth century. Georgian buildings, which were erected from about 1700 to 1783, were the true "Colonials." There are outstanding examples along the East Coast, notably in Portsmouth and Exeter, New Hampshire; Marblehead and Salem, Massachusetts; Newport, Rhode Island; Annapolis, Maryland; Charleston, South Carolina; and, of course, Williamsburg, capital of Virginia until 1780.

The style in the American colonies was derivative: it came from contemporary British buildings, which were inspired by the Italian Renaissance, which descended from ancient Roman architecture, which in turn emulated the work of the Greeks. This is the way with much of the history of architecture.

A Georgian house was formal with a generally symmetrical front façade. The *focal point* was the entrance, which was embellished with the fanciest *portico* the owner could afford.

Because the glass industry was primitive, small panes with irregularities were set into twelve over twelve or nine over nine windows (this means that the top *sashes* held nine panes of glass and the bottom sashes held nine panes of glass) and later six over six windows. This is also depicted as 6/6.

The Haven Parsonage (not shown here) on Rochester Hill Road, an example of Georgian architecture, is believed to be the oldest intact building in Rochester. The house was erected in 1760 for Parson Amos Main, whose statue stands in Central Square downtown. It is a popular notion, but probably an "urban" legend, that Main Street was named after him.

# Federal Architecture

When the Revolutionary War ended in 1783, we wished to assert our independence in fashion as well as governance, and the term "Georgian" was no longer appropriate. The "Federal" style arose. Our newfound national pride notwithstanding, this style, like Georgian, came directly from Britain. There, it was called Adamesque after two Scottish architect brothers who traveled to Italy to inspect Roman architecture firsthand, bypassing the Renaissance middleman this time.

*High-style* Federal houses often incorporate the urns, sheaves of wheat and *swags* that were uncovered in structures in Pompeii and the circular and oval rooms found in Roman palaces. Entrances are often flanked by *sidelights* and surmounted by a *fanlight*. The style is more delicate than Georgian, but the differences may be subtle, particularly in *vernacular* buildings.

Many of the most elegant examples, including attached brick town houses, are found in Portland, Maine; Salem and Boston's Beacon Hill in Massachusetts; Providence, Rhode Island; New York City; New Haven, Connecticut; Baltimore, Maryland; Richmond, Virginia; and Savannah, Georgia. Newburyport, Massachusetts, has an incomparable collection of Federal mansions, many on High Street, which I think is one of the most beautiful streets in the country.

Pattern books of building *elevations* and house plans became popular in the nineteenth century and facilitated the spread of new styles. One of the first was Asher Benjamin's *The American Builder's Companion*, published in 1798, which promoted the new Federal architecture. This style faded about 1830.

## Old Dover Road

The stately Colonel John McDuffee House was built circa 1779. This Georgian house is noteworthy for its *gambrel* roof, large center chimney, 9/6 windows, narrow clapboards and delicate entry *portico* with four *lights* in the *transom* window over the door.

According to John Moscone, the owner, a cannon that had been set up on Haven Hill, now Rochester Hill, sounded when the Battle of Bunker Hill began. John McDuffee, a veteran of numerous battles in the French and Indian War, saddled his horse and rode to Charlestown, Massachusetts, in

Old Dover Road

Rochester Hill Road

one day to join the struggle. He fought in several more battles and was with General Washington throughout the Valley Forge Campaign. McDuffie returned to Rochester, building this house when he was fifty-four years old. He lived to the age of ninety-seven. Mr. Moscone describes him as "one fighting son of a gun."

## ROCHESTER HILL ROAD

Haven House, not the Haven Parsonage, is not a Federal-era structure, but it was built in the Federal style a number of years later. This is a grand property, but one in need of rejuvenation. It once overlooked a wide expanse of open land, but it is now circumscribed by subsequent subdivision. The site features a fine post and beam barn, a small horse paddock, a well-worn fountain, eighty-foot-tall pines, hoary old maples and rows of ancient cedar trees.

# THE GREEK REVIVAL STYLE

*Greek architecture is the flowering of geometry.*
—*Ralph Waldo Emerson*

In the early nineteenth century, the American public was captivated by archaeological excavations in Greece and that country's war of independence against the Ottoman Turks. We identified with their ancient experiment in self rule and current struggle for freedom. New towns with names like Athens, Ithaca, Sparta and Corinth arose across the country.

The Greek Revival style was popular in the 1830s and 1840s. Banks, state capitols, churches and homes displayed temple fronts with columns or *pilasters*. *High-style* buildings, such as those on Tara—the plantation, not the mobile home park in Rochester—display a full porch with four, six or eight freestanding columns.

The achievements of early Greece in architecture, art, literature, theatre, philosophy and astronomy form the foundation of much of Western culture. The Greeks were aesthetes seeking an eternal truth. They spent one hundred years refining the *Doric* order (these were not "blow and go" developers!) culminating in the Parthenon. There is genius in this building. The columns exhibit *entasis*, which is a subtle bulge incorporated just below the middle to counteract the eye's natural perception of a straight column as being slightly concave. The columns also lean slightly toward the center to convey a feeling of repose and they are slightly thicker and placed slightly closer together at the corners to visually anchor the building.

Salmon Falls
Road

Mathematicians have studied the Parthenon and find a complex series of *golden sections* embodied in the façade. The golden section is a proportion that human beings seem to find innately satisfying. It is the ratio of approximately 5 to 8, or precisely 1 to 1.618…, an irrational mathematical constant, like pi (ruminate on this concept: the number continues indefinitely without any patterns!). Systems of proportion like this one are based on the belief that certain numerical relationships manifest the harmonic structure of the universe.[*] Jonathan Hale, a writer about traditional design, sees these proportions in Audrey Hepburn's face.[†] Now, I'm sold.

By the way, a *proportion* is the relationship of one dimension to another, usually expressed as a ratio, such as 1:3, or as a fraction, such as 1/3. A window, for example, that is one foot wide and five feet high (1:5) would have elongated proportions. When one speaks of a building having "good proportions," this means that the various individual ratios—of the windows, of the overall height and width of the façade, of the overall area of windows to wall space, etc.—are harmonious with one another. *Scale* is the size of a building or an element of a building relative to the size of a specific standard, usually the human body. Scale is not generally calculated precisely; rather, one typically speaks of "large scale" or "small scale."

---

[*] Ching, *Architecture*, 300.
[†] Hale, *The Old Way of Seeing*, 68.

# Horizontal and Vertical Elements

Greek Revival architecture uses strong vertical and horizontal elements, along with the contrasting diagonal *pediment*. The Greeks were familiar with the arch but never used it in a visible way. In contrast, the Romans used the arch with bravura, in coliseums, aqueducts, viaducts and public baths. They also exploited the *vault* and the dome.

The Greek (and Greek Revival) orders function like sub-styles specifying standards for columns and *entablatures*. *Doric*, the oldest order, is relatively simple and massive. The column rests directly on the platform without a base and the *capital* is essentially a simple plate. All of the houses shown here have *Doric* columns or *pilasters*.

The more attenuated *Ionic* column stands on a pedestal and is crowned by a volute, i.e., a scroll, a ram's horn, an upside-down handlebar mustache or, shall we say, the whorl of a gastropod shell. The ancient Roman architect Vitruvius wrote that the Ionic form evokes a woman with its slender profile and volutes recalling a woman's curls, like a pageboy haircut.

The *Corinthian capital* displays an overflowing of *acanthus* leaves. According to Vitruvius, a young lady from Corinth died and her nurse laid a basket with her possessions on her tomb. An acanthus plant grew around the basket. Some time later, the Athenian sculptor Callimachus passed the tomb and was moved by the sight. He then modeled a new *capital* after it.[*] The acanthus leaf is also used to decorate graves.

Rochester Hill Road-1

---

[*] Mouzon, *Traditional Construction Patterns*, 54–56.

The Erechtheion is a temple on the Acropolis, the complex of buildings outside of Athens that includes the Parthenon. Its columns are standing women called *caryatids*. This device is a natural transposition, as the column evokes the erect human body with its base (foot), shaft (legs and torso) and *capital* (head). The Greeks also had a lesser used male version, called *atlantes*.

### Salmon Falls Road

The *portico* with the heavy granite steps below and delicate light over the door is beautifully *proportioned*. There are simplified *entablatures* over the door and under the *eaves*.

### Rochester Hill Road-1

This house has two nearly matching, five-*bay* façades. This is a good example of a *pediment* at the top on the left façade. Note the *sidelight* shutters along the entrances.

### Rochester Hill Road-2

This structure is unusual for the placement of its entrance on the long side, within a cutaway corner. I would love to replace those columns with a trio of caryatids to greet passing motorists.

Traditionally, Greek Revival buildings have been painted white, like this one, under the mistaken idea that the ancient temples were white. The originals were constructed of white marble, but they were painted many vivid colors, which had long since worn off by the time modern Europeans rediscovered them!

Rochester
Hill Road-2

# THE ITALIANATE STYLE

*You may have the universe if I may have Italy.*
*—Guiseppe Verdi*

## Victorian Styles

Queen Victoria ruled England from 1837 to 1901, a total of sixty-four years. Most nineteenth-century western architecture after Greek Revival is considered Victorian. This period embodied a remarkable, even frenetic, exploration of one historical style after another.

A number of Victorian styles were born in the Picturesque movement in Britain, which was a reaction to the formal *neoclassical* styles that preceded it—Georgian, Federal and Greek Revival, as they were called in this country. These picturesque designs exhibited asymmetry, steep roofs, multiple colors and multiple textures.

Industrial development and expansion of the railroads facilitated the growth of Victorian styles. Balloon frame construction, using two-inch-thick boards fastened together with wire nails, replaced the use of heavy timbers. This lighter method of building allowed for flexibility in layouts. Building components could also be mass produced and shipped economically all over the country.

# Gothic Revival

One of the first Victorian fashions was Gothic Revival, which emerged in the 1830s. This romantic style, in residential as opposed to *ecclesiastical* architecture, was promoted in the book *Cottage Residences*, which was a collaboration between architect Alexander Jackson Davis and landscape designer Andrew Jackson Downing (can you believe those names?). There are no true Gothic Revival houses in Rochester, but a handful evoke the style with their steep roofs and *cross gables*.

# Palladio

The Italianate style of architecture followed, and was popular from about 1850 to 1880. Designers found inspiration in villas and rambling farmhouses in the countryside of northern Italy.

The most handsome of those Italian villas were designed by Andrea Palladio (Signor not Signora) during the Renaissance. Many consider him the most influential architect of all time, for both his buildings and his treatise, *The Four Books of Architecture*. Andrea diPietro was dubbed Palladio in homage to Pallas Athena, the Greek goddess of wisdom.

This great architect suffers the ignominious fate of having his name now attached to the most conspicuous feature of the contemporary McMansion: the *Palladian window*, which is a triple window with an arch over the central window. Indeed, he did originate, or at least refine, this motif, but he rendered it with grace.

The Italianate style is distinctive for its use of broad, overhanging *eaves* with decorative *brackets*; round-headed windows and doors; *hoods* over windows; square and hexagonal *bay windows*; corner *quoins*; and, on elaborate examples, *towers* and *cupolas*.

This style is highly adaptable to different building types. In spite of its bucolic roots, Italianate is the prevalent design used for downtown commercial buildings in the small American cities that bloomed in the decades after the Civil War. Rochester grew significantly in this period. Mill owners and their managers erected fashionable residences on the main corridors branching out of downtown: Wakefield, North and South Main, Charles and Portland Streets. Merchants, craftsmen and millworkers built more modest homes on the side streets.

# Architectural Styles

Heaton Street

Knight Street

Virtually all Georgian and Federal structures were oriented with the gable toward the side, i.e., the roof ridge and long side of the house were placed parallel to the street. The Greek Revival house, with its temple front, turned the gable ninety degrees to face forward. The subsequent Italianate style maintained this orientation, which was convenient for houses sited on narrow and deep in-town lots.

Admittedly, it is striking how different the following three examples look from one another, particularly with their distinct roof forms. Each displays one or two strong Italianate elements: a *bay window* and projecting *eaves, brackets* and round-headed windows, respectively.

## HEATON STREET

This dwelling is notable for its low pitched roof and broad *eaves*, those demure mini-*brackets* at the upper corners, elaborate scrollwork supporting the entry canopy and wood cladding scored to resemble stone.

## KNIGHT STREET

This marvelous house is a riot of *dentils* and *brackets*.

## MAIN STREET, GONIC

The Whitehouse house is the grande dame of Gonic, a village on the southwesterly side of Rochester. Sitting at the head of Main Street, the house *terminates the vista* memorably as you drive toward the small downtown. The structure is noteworthy for its massive, boxlike form; superb *cupola* with

Main Street, Gonic

intact *finial; fluted Corinthian* columns in the entry; and arched shutters. The property was clad in vinyl after this photograph was taken.

This eclectic building could easily be designated Second Empire. However, it is presented here because it displays a number of strong Italianate features. Therefore, I must instruct you to pay no attention to that mansard roof on the top.

# THE SECOND EMPIRE STYLE

*If you are lucky enough to have lived in Paris as a young man, then wherever you
go for the rest of your life, it stays with you, for Paris is a moveable feast.*
—*Ernest Hemingway*

The Second Empire style originated in France in the mid-nineteenth
century during the reign of Emperor Napoleon III. He sought to
rekindle his nation's former glory under the first emperor, Napoleon
Bonaparte.

Napoleon III hired engineer Georges-Eugène Haussmann, who called
himself Baron Haussmann (he was a baron in the same way that Elvis's
manager "Colonel" Tom Parker was a colonel), and granted him enormous
powers to remake the city. These powers were similar to those conferred on
Robert Moses in New York City one hundred years later. Both aggressively
pushed through large-*scale* roads, but whereas Moses's legacy is one of
highways devastating neighborhoods, Haussmann transformed Paris into
one of the most beautiful cities in the world.

Baron Haussmann developed many of the city's glorious boulevards;
established a public transportation system with horse-drawn buses; built
aqueducts and sewers; and created open spaces around, and vistas toward,
monuments like the Arc de Triomphe and the Opera House, all similar to
projects we have going in Rochester.

Haussmann decreed in 1852 that houses situated on a boulevard were
limited to six stories (a wise proclamation, as this height reinforces proper
scale on the city's grand thoroughfares). Clever developers managed to sneak

Grant Street

in a usable seventh floor by increasing the pitch of the attic to nearly vertical. This style of roof had been popularized two hundred years earlier by the seventeenth-century French architect François Mansart.

The *mansard* roof (after Mansart), the hallmark of Second Empire, has a double pitch: a steep lower section, sometimes called a *skirt*, and a shallow upper section, usually not visible from the street. The skirt is commonly straight or concave in profile, as seen looking along the side of the roof. There are *high-style* examples with convex roofs. For some peculiar reason, the only new mansard roofs one sees today are on fast-food restaurants. The establishments call them "mansard roofs," but actually they are usually inverted, with the shallow slope below and the steep slope above. Very chic.

The Second Empire style was popular in Europe and America during the 1860s and early 1870s. It was sometimes called the Mansard style or the General Grant style, having coincided with the Civil War. Second Empire fell out of favor after the defeat of France in the 1870 Franco-Prussian War and the economic panic of 1873, with the accompanying decline of Paris as the center of fashion.

The four-story brick McDuffee Block (shown in the mural), rendered in the Second Empire style, was described in the city's 1982 cultural survey as "unquestionably the most significant structure in Rochester." At 2:00 a.m. on April 15, 1992, while heading back after dousing another fire, the Rochester Fire Department learned that the McDuffee Block was ablaze. Tragically, it could not be saved, the victim of a casual act of arson.

### GRANT STREET
The St. Charles Children's Home was built in 1878 as the residence of Edwin Wallace, one of the owners of the Wallace Shoe Company. This building displays a *polygonal tower*, *pedimented* window heads on the second floor, dormers partly recessed into the roof and an ornate porch.

St. Charles was founded as an orphanage in 1913. In 1968, it was converted into a transitional home for young children from families in crisis. It is staffed by the Daughters of Mary, Mother of Healing Love, a religious association of women, consecrated as sisters.

### SOUTH MAIN STREET
The Emily Cross House, built in 1865, has a profusion of detail, including *dentils*, corner *quoins* and a wraparound porch with curlicue *brackets* on the

South Main Street

35

posts. Local CPA Don Carignan carried out an outstanding restoration of the house using the federal historic rehabilitation investment tax credit.

This tool allows for a 20 percent <u>credit</u> of the total renovation costs, reducing one's tax burden dollar for dollar (versus a less valuable <u>deduction</u>). This credit may be used for a business or rental property that is listed on, or deemed eligible for, the National Register of Historic Places. One must rehabilitate the outside and inside to the standards of the United States Secretary of the Interior. No doubt, Don was not intimidated by the program's complex accounting procedures.

# The Queen Anne Style

*Exuberance is beauty.*
*—William Blake*

If the Victorians were repressed in manners, they compensated in the vivacity of their architecture. The creativity seen throughout the nineteenth century—in styles such as Gothic, Italianate, Octagon and Moorish, Turkish and Egyptian Revival—culminated in the effervescence of Queen Anne. This style is the high-water mark for personality and richness of design in the history of American architecture.

The Queen Anne style was characterized by a cornucopia of towers, turrets, spindles and spools. Simplicity and symmetry were eschewed. Overlapping geometric shapes obscured the basic form of the building. A mix of finishes, colors and materials—brick, stone, terra cotta, iron, copper and wood—brought an intricate texture. The interiors incorporated sumptuous dark woods and offered secretive nooks and alcoves. Surprisingly, it was conservative bankers, physicians and industrialists who built these homes and relished living in them.

If you come upon an extravagant, "over-the-top" old house that seems to defy placement into one of the standard styles, just go ahead and call it Queen Anne. But say it with confidence.

Don't ask what all of this has to do with Queen Anne herself. I have no idea. The architectural style was popular from 1880 to 1900, toward the end of Queen Victoria's reign, whereas Queen Anne ruled Britain from 1702 to 1714, during a period of rather formal architecture. I see no evidence

King Street

Kimball Street

Wakefield Street-1

that she was particularly animated herself. In fact, Queen Anne suffered unthinkable tragedy: she was pregnant eighteen times, and the only child who lived beyond the age of two succumbed at eleven.

# Shingle Style

The Shingle style was a variant of Queen Anne. It reached its apogee in the large "cottages" of Newport, Rhode Island; Cape Cod, Massachusetts; and other seaside resorts in the Northeast, where the effect was one of a continuous skin of wood shingles enclosing a complex, swelling mass. The shingle can be readily shaped around curving forms and cut into patterns, such as diamonds, fish scales and saw teeth. There are no pure examples of the Shingle style in Rochester, but it is evoked in many houses here that exhibit a fantastic use of shingles.

# The Rochester Fair

There are several fine original Queen Anne buildings in the Rochester Fairgrounds complex (not shown here). Come check out these structures and visit the fair, which is held for ten days each September. The Rochester Fair opened in 1874 and is the oldest and one of the most entertaining fairs in New Hampshire. It offers amusement park rides, circuses, pig racing, monster trucks, demolition derbies, tractor pulls, lumberjack competitions, giant pumpkins, farm animals, cotton candy and live country music. The fair will put you in a Queen Anne state of mind.

### KING STREET
This house displays an intricate massing and an abundance of charming details: a sunburst, an oriel window (a projecting *bay window* raised above ground level) and grooved porch posts and *newel posts*. At the same time, though, it has a certain unexpected modesty about it.

### KIMBALL STREET
Yes, this building is real and "profusion" is the word. It actually is two dwellings that were linked together. The property owner has my number. Whenever I see him, he jokingly (I hope) tells me that he is thinking about putting siding on the structure.

*Above*: Cocheco Avenue

*Left*: Wakefield Street-2

## Wakefield Street-1

Gaze at that *tower* on the right. It is spectacular. Unfortunately, you cannot appreciate its lovely powder blue, coral and off white colors. You will have to have a look when you come to the fair.

## Cocheco Avenue

This extraordinary house displays those eccentric eyelids over each window, curvilinear aprons under each window, cutaway corner windows on the second floor and four different shingle patterns. The house is owned by Dewey Faulhaber, owner of Pegleg Canes, who makes artistic walking canes. It was built in 1882 by a dry goods store owner. The house is currently for sale, and Dewey told me that the realtor was advertising it as a colonial!

## Wakefield Street-2

There are various pairs of contrasting elements here: clapboards and shingles; flush and flared wall sections; a projecting *bay* set against a flat background wall; a three-story *bay* that is partly angled and partly square; and that flowerbox jawing at a complementary brow above.

Bravo to the owners of these structures for maintaining the original wood cladding materials. When the vinyl siding salesman comes knocking on the door of your historic home, send him on his way. You will preserve the character and value of your house, and continue to delight the neighbors as well.

# THE COLONIAL REVIVAL STYLE

*Why is it that a man just as soon as he gets enough money,*
*builds a house much bigger than he needs?*
—*Harvey Firestone, founder of Firestone Tire and Rubber Company*

The Queen Anne style was excessive in its creative abandon. The Colonial Revival style, which followed close behind, was often simply excessive. The style revived the Georgian fashion, but many traditional features, including dormers, *cornerboards* and *porticos*, as well as the form of the overall house itself, were exaggerated, if not grandiose, in *scale*.

The Philadelphia Centennial Exposition in 1876 aroused interest in our country's pre-Revolutionary history. This enthusiasm was expressed a number of years later in the Colonial Revival style, which flowered in the 1890s and continued in various permutations into the early decades of the twentieth century and beyond.

The Colonial Revival dwelling was typically configured like the traditional Georgian house, with a simple rectangular plan and the wider side of the house facing the street. Most examples have five *bays* arranged symmetrically around a center door, like the Broad Street dwelling, below. Some *high-style* examples, however, such as the Wakefield Street structure, below, were influenced by the complex massing of the contemporaneous Queen Anne style and departed from this basic layout.

# Sumner Wallace House

Rochester's greatest Colonial Revival structure was the Sumner Wallace House, built in 1901, on South Main Street. It had twenty large rooms, a ballroom on the entire top floor and a wide *porte-cochère*. The house was the headquarters of the New Hampshire Ku Klux Klan from 1924 to 1927. The burning cross, which the Klan maintained on the roof, must have been a shocking sight.

I wonder if the wizards of the KKK knew that they were neighbors to a former station on the Underground Railroad, located diagonally across the street. The Underground Railroad was a network of safe houses, or "stations," established in the mid-1800s to secretly move escaped slaves from the South all the way to Canada. Susan Edgerly, proprietor of Edgerly Funeral Home, at 86 South Main Street, told me she believes that the earlier Edgerly house on her property was a station.

Regrettably, the Sumner Wallace House was demolished in 1932. As a side note, the Ku Klux Klan came to New Hampshire not to harass African Americans—whose numbers were, and still are, negligible in the state—but rather to challenge the growing influx of Catholics from Quebec.

# Rochester Historic District—A Short Detour

Let us digress briefly to discuss the historic district. Much of Rochester's downtown is a National Register District, a federal designation that provides virtually no protection for listed properties. It is the local historic district, adopted by city ordinance, that prevents inappropriate changes. The Historic District Commission (HDC) adheres to a set of standards, but the commission may exercise discretion, since each property and each proposal is unique.

The HDC, composed of local citizens, has authority to approve or deny new construction, additions, alterations or demolitions within the district. It has purview only over portions of the exterior of buildings that are visible from a public way. Approval is required for new activities that the property owner initiates; existing conditions are considered "grandfathered." Creative contemporary designs are not discouraged provided they are compatible with the historic fabric.

# Architectural Styles

Broad Street

Wakefield Street

## Broad Street

In this seasonal photograph, former Mayor Harvey and Karen Bernier adorned their house with wreaths, window boxes and *festoons*. The stately *hip roof* and tall chimneys contrast with the simple entry and delicately *proportioned broken swan's neck pediment.* Note the slightly shorter second-floor windows.

## Wakefield Street

Harvey Bernier is the king of Colonial Revival. He operates Bernier Insurance out of this 1905 dwelling. This structure is the city's most *high-style* extant Colonial Revival house, with its large *hip roof, bow* and *bay windows,* curving wraparound porch, oversized dormer and *Palladian window.* Lest the building get too highfalutin, though, Harvey offers changing displays of mischievous yard and roof ornaments, including magical zinnias, daffy penguins and sloshed snowmen.

# The Foursquare Style

*The strength of a nation is derived from the integrity of its homes.*
*—Confucius*

Foursquare. It's a children's game (and, I am also told, a Lutheran hymn). The name is modest, and redundant, I might add, and the style is not widely recognized, but it is distinctive.

Foursquare houses are roughly square in plan (you could have guessed that) with a *hip roof*. If the house is perfectly square with the same slope on all sides, the roof ends in a point. Many Foursquare dwellings are not exactly square, and thus have a short ridge at the top.

The typical Foursquare has two stories and seems nearly cubic in volume. The dwelling's simplicity, in both shape and ornamentation, was a break from the increasingly elaborate designs of the prior half century. Foursquare houses were constructed using pattern books or were prefabricated and sold through catalogues such as Sears & Roebuck's. The base price for the Chelsea model, for example, an attractive two-story home, was $943 in 1914 (roughly equivalent to $20,000 in 2009 dollars).

## Progressive Era

The form echoes the dictionary meaning of the word "foursquare": "marked by firm or unwavering conviction, forthright and candid." This character was reflected at the time in the quality of housing, streets, neighborhoods

Church Street

and government. The first few decades of the twentieth century, when Foursquare was in vogue, were known as the Progressive Era. This period saw the city planning movement become firmly established under the visionary leadership of architects such as Chicago's Daniel Burnham, who is credited with having said, "Make no little plans. They have no magic to stir men's blood."

Many developments were designed with parks, squares and rear alleys, the latter a brilliant device that has been revived by the new urbanists. A rear alley (or the more agreeable "service lane") allows for placement of less attractive elements—automobiles, driveways, utilities and garbage—out of view of the street.

Wide-ranging civic improvements were made in this period, including planting of the majestic trees that lined America's most graceful neighborhoods. Craig Turnbull, author of a book about this era, said,

> *Urban landscapes of the late nineteenth and early twentieth centuries were shaped by an ideology of "improvement" that resonated throughout the United States...based on an assumption that built environments reflected and shaped the moral, political, and cultural character of individuals and*

*Left*: Pickering Road

*Below*: Academy Street

*communities... The growing number of improved residential landscapes in Chicago after 1890 were visually distinguished by features such as well-maintained, paved streets and sidewalks; street lamps; and street trees.*\*

A robust street tree program used to be a source of pride for many communities. In addition to their various environmental contributions, street trees add beauty to neighborhoods and enhance property values. Consider how the loss of trees to disease (most notoriously, Dutch elm disease in the mid-twentieth century), lack of maintenance or road widening devastates the quality of a street. It is heartbreaking to see old postcards of South Main and Wakefield Streets under a splendid arcade of elm trees. They are now mostly gone.

## Church Street

This handsome dwelling near downtown Gonic is the quintessential Foursquare with its full-width porch, shallow two-story *bay windows* and dormers with double windows. As far as we know, ours is the only Gonic in the entire world. It is the abbreviated version of the Indian name Squamanagonic, which means "the water of the clay place hill." Quite poetic.

## Pickering Road

This sturdy Foursquare, shrouded in ivy and vegetation, has an ethereal beauty.

## Academy Street

The interior of this 1915 house is a sensation. The original owner commissioned painters, sculptors and craftsmen to embellish the walls and ceilings throughout. Square-masted galleons plot a course through the hallway. Ladies in kimonos, luxuriant flowers and Mount Fuji adorn the Japanese room. Another space is rendered in an English baronial style. In the French room, cherubs are cavorting in the manner of Louis XIV, the Sun King. How about that? A touch of Versailles right here in Rochester, New Hampshire.

---

\* Turnbull, *An American Urban Residential Landscape.*

# Other Twentieth-Century House Styles

*No house should ever be on a hill or on anything. It should be of the hill.*
*Belonging to it. Hill and house should live together each the happier for the other.*
*—Frank Lloyd Wright*

The twentieth century witnessed numerous new styles and rediscoveries, but nothing like the cavalcade of revivals in the nineteenth century. Since World War II, no particular style has dominated, particularly in domestic design, as the American architectural scene has largely been an inarticulate muddle.

## Tudor Revival

The Tudor Revival style, which overlapped with the Foursquare style, enjoyed a distinguished revival in the 1920s, particularly in affluent suburbs outside of New York and Boston, such as Scarsdale, Newton and Winchester. There is one noteworthy Tudor Revival–style ranch in Rochester on North Main Street, just beyond Strafford Square.

The name is an anachronism, like "Queen Anne." "Tudor" refers to the royal house that ruled Britain during the Renaissance, but it was the earlier medieval period that inspired the look. A side theme for this chapter could be elements and expressions that are out of place, out of time or out of character. I offer here a ramble among middle and late twentieth-century houses in Rochester.

Rochester Hill
Road-1

## ROCHESTER HILL ROAD-1

This Mediterranean-style house from 1939 is the city's only example of the style. I wonder about its inspiration, as this style is common in Florida and the West. The defining features include the red clay tiled roof, arched entry block, bull's-eye and oval windows, *casement windows* and a small terrace on the right. According to the owner, the buff brick, roof tiles and interior redwood roof rafters were imported from California, which is impressive for a modestly *scaled* house built at the close of the Depression.

## ROCHESTER HILL ROAD-2

This 1948 neo-Gothic house demonstrates how a single design element can transform the character of a structure. Broad reincarnations of an older style are generally called "revivals" and isolated individual examples or fleeting reincarnations are often labeled "neo," which means "new." The steeply pitched entry with its fine brickwork lends an intrigue from the Middle Ages to an otherwise straightforward house. The entry also displays a rare *compound arch*. The awnings are perfect, and how about that Gothic shrub at the corner, shaped like a *pointed arch*!

## SUNSET DRIVE

The Hillcrest-Sunset neighborhood has a fine trove of distinctive houses from the 1950s and 1960s. This brown house, built about forty years ago, is a good example of what is still called the "contemporary" style.

# Architectural Styles

Rochester Hill Road-2

Sunset Drive

The style emphasized natural materials, gently sloping roofs, exposed beams, skylights and decks and patios in the rear, all of which serve to echo the landscape. The interiors of contemporary houses often have a large hearth at the center, an open floor plan, dark wood and a cathedral ceiling, albeit a low one. Awning windows (opened from the top) were common.

The house has a recumbent quality that is made more dramatic by the towering trees behind it. The dwelling does display some vertical character as well, in the chimney and glass block window, reflecting the wooded setting in which these houses were often placed.

## GLORIA STREET

Ranch houses first became popular in the 1940s as the rising use of automobiles opened up the suburbs to development. Land was cheaper, and houses could spread out on their lots.

There is no established name for this style, so I am going to call this house a Sixties Streamlined Ranch. There are several houses of this type around Rochester, especially in the Roy-Madison Street neighborhood, sided variously in masonite, asbestos or oversized cedar shingles. Horizontality is stressed here in the windows, landscaping, low-slung profile, double-width garage door, knife edge *eaves* and even the open brickwork of the chimney. I don't ordinarily get this excited about double-width garage doors.

## QUARRY DRIVE

This picturesque house, built in 1992, with its multiple steep gables, aspiring chimney, *casement windows* and two-story *bay window* tucked in at the corner, evokes an English manor house. The *Tudor arch* at the entry is a nice touch. Certain Teed, a high-quality brand of siding, is used here successfully. This is the last time you will hear me exclaim enthusiastically about vinyl siding.

## ROCKLEDGE ROAD

This superbly landscaped 1995 property recalls a formal English country estate. Though asymmetrical, it is skillfully balanced around the off-center entrance. The three massive, front-facing gables are mitigated by windows broken into small squares, and the expansive roof is separated into upper and lower sections. This house has no pretense of understatement, so I do not begrudge its audacious deployment of, not one, but two palatial Palladian windows.

*Opposite, top*: Gloria Street
*Opposite, middle*: Quarry Drive
*Opposite, bottom*: Rockledge Road

# Contemporary
# Commercial Designs

*In Houston, a person walking is somebody on the way to their car.*
*—Anthony Downs, public policy scholar*

## Contemporary Design

Much contemporary commercial architecture is regrettable. There are numerous reasons for this. The quality of the experience, and therefore architectural quality, is important in a pedestrian environment because walking takes a long time. For those driving to their destination, the impact of the buildings is reduced, particularly when they are situated behind a large parking lot.

Businesses emphasize commercial branding with their buildings, promoting a homogeneous, packaged image. There is a diminution of corporate citizenship and commitment to the local community, with chains from out of state dominating in many markets. Developers and businesses are less willing to pay the small, additional increment for high-quality architecture. Most of the architectural schools are not even teaching traditional design principles any longer, so the creations of many architects are of questionable appeal.

Entire structures or significant portions of structures are now being manufactured in factories. Metals and plastics are increasingly replacing the use of wood and brick. There is a pervasive fear of liability, a reluctance of the public sector to press for good design out of concern about encroaching on private property rights and, in general, a public that has come to accept mediocrity in design.

Fortunately, many communities are resisting these trends, and various chains have produced pleasing new prototypes. McDonald's is redeveloping one of its older sites in town. There will be arches on the building, to be sure, but they are understated, even hip, like Nike swooshes. The company showcases its versatility around the country with Mediterranean-style McDonald's in Florida, Mission-style McDonald's in New Mexico and Prairie-style McDonald's in the Midwest.

# Architectural Regulations

Rochester adopted architectural regulations that apply to all new commercial and multifamily buildings throughout the city. The provisions are similar to those in effect in our historic district, as principles of good design apply to old and new structures alike.

Well-crafted standards can bring forth buildings that are functional, economical and attractive. The City of Rochester discourages building designs that are indifferent to the traditions of the region, aggressively seek the attention of passing motorists, do not consider the quality of the pedestrian environment or are erected at the lowest possible cost without due concern for aesthetics.

The following structures are all relatively new. The first three illustrate how a simple, one-story building can be enriched with architectural elements that are integral to the structure rather than having the feel of being gratuitously tacked on.

## South Main Street
The Ocean Bank building is impressive for its materials, colors, landscaping, signage and *fenestration*. That means windows. I know, I know, but why say "windows" when you can say "fenestration"?

## North Main Street
Burger King recently redeveloped this property. The design is simple but has strong elements: a pronounced *cornice*, copper-colored metal awnings, high-quality brick and a corner *tower*.

# Architectural Styles

South Main Street

North Main Street

### FARMINGTON ROAD-1

This new prototype for Pizza Hut is enlivened with a nicely designed *frontispiece*, awnings, variations in colors and materials and a high *hip roof* crowned by an unusual raised block.

### FARMINGTON ROAD-2

The frontage of the Shoe Department shopping plaza, with its covered arcade, is reminiscent of a traditional downtown. The piers and light poles create a satisfying rhythm.

### FARMINGTON ROAD-3

This Granite Ford building is evocative of the 1930s Streamline Moderne style with its curved corners. It is clad in "EIFS" (□'-f□s), which stands for exterior insulating finishing system. This material, which resembles stucco, is popular now with builders. EIFS is a veneer, only about 1/16 of an inch thick, but it is fairly durable. The striations break up the mass of the façade effectively.

I couldn't resist shooting this terrific 1930 Ford Model A. It is owned by Ryan Thibeau, a mechanical engineering student, who maintains the car himself (the original engine is partially rebuilt). Many contemporary commercial buildings are erected with the expectation that they will be razed within a few decades. The developers seem to acknowledge, from the outset, the unworthiness of their creations. In contrast, Ryan boldly spurs on his seventy-nine-year-old vehicle at fifty-five miles per hour on the highway.

*Opposite, top*: Farmington Road-1
*Opposite, middle*: Farmington Road-2
*Opposite, bottom*: Farmington Road-3

# MODERNISM

*Modern architects recognize 300 masterpieces but ignore the other 30 million buildings that have ruined the world.*
*—Andres Duany*

Mr. Duany, one of the leaders of the New Urbanism movement, is referring to modernist architects. His numbers might be slightly skewed. At any rate, I find the story of modernism to be fascinating.

## The Bauhaus

In the 1920s, amid the tumult following World War I, American writers, artists and architects traveled to Europe seeking a deeper truth. The Bauhaus school in Weimar, Germany, led by architectural guru Walter Gropius, was a magnet for these searchers.

The Bauhaus renounced old Europe and anything considered "bourgeois." Traditional architecture was verboten; the mantra was "starting from zero." Gropius declared, "We want to create…[an] architecture, whose inner logic will be radiant and naked, unencumbered by lying façades and trickeries; we want an architecture adapted to our world of machines, radios and fast motor cars."*

Le Corbusier, one of the high priests of modernism, famously stated, "A house is a machine for living."

---

* Wolfe, *From Bauhaus to Our House*, ch. 1.

The leitmotif of the Bauhaus was authenticity, purity and simplicity. It embraced the principle "form follows function," from "form <u>ever</u> follows function," asserted by Chicago architect Louis Sullivan, practicing a generation earlier. Applied ornamentation—like the *porticos* and *pediments* of *classical* architecture—was considered superfluous and even unmanly. Sullivan relished applying delicate terra cotta patterns to his skyscrapers, but I doubt his vigor was ever questioned.

The new architecture was to transcend style, time—hence "modernism"— and place, hence "the International style," as it came to be known. Le Corbusier proposed razing the heart of Paris and replacing it with a complex of towers set into parks and linked by superhighways. A charming idea.

## Plain Boxes

Ludwig Mies van der Rohe (or simply "Mies") summed it up, proclaiming, "Less is more." The result was gleaming white boxes and industrial-type buildings with exposed structural elements made of steel, glass, concrete and stucco. Mies was a perfectionist. He also said, "God is in the details." Like a number of modernist architects who publicly shunned traditional design and enrichment, Mies lived in a *high-style* Victorian house. But lest his commitment to the cause be questioned, he painted the entire exterior pure white.

There are extraordinary modernist buildings in this country. Mies's high-rise Seagram Building in Manhattan and Farnsworth House (a glass house in Plano, Illinois) are breathtakingly beautiful in their materials and *proportions*. The problem with this stripped-down approach, however, is that there is only so much you can do with a plain box. After a while, particularly when rendered by lesser talents than Mies, plain boxes are plain ugly. In response to Mies's "Less is more," architect Robert Venturi later averred, "Less is a bore."

The elements of this functionalism—lack of ornament, a flat roof, use of "ribbons" of horizontal windows, expanses of blank wall, inconspicuous entrances—became its own aesthetic, just another design style, like all that came before. Plus, modernism's functionalism turned out not to be so

*Opposite, top*: South Main Street-1
*Opposite, middle*: Wakefield Street
*Opposite, bottom*: South Main Street-2

# Architectural Styles

functional: flat roofs leak and people get frustrated trying to find the front door of a building. In their compulsion to renounce tradition for sheer functionalism, the modernists failed to see that many traditions had arisen out of practical solutions to problems.

Notwithstanding my comments above, well-executed modernist buildings are captivating. Here are three noteworthy examples.

## SOUTH MAIN STREET-1

Several additions behind the Rochester Public Library are different in style but visually tied together by use of red brick. The entry block, built in 1997, shuns traditional patterns: a metal strip serves as the *cornice*, there is a broad expanse of blank wall, the wall planes do not meet and the windows are unbroken by *muntins*. Yet this is an elegant piece of modernist architectural sculpture.

## WAKEFIELD STREET

This particular 1960 subtype of the style features colored metal rectangular panels. The aluminum grid and the panels it holds in place is a decorative front evoking the image of an exposed structural skeleton. Modernism preached honest expression of structure, but over time acquired its own affectations. I applaud Federal Savings Bank for its excellent recent renovation of this building.

## SOUTH MAIN STREET-2

This structure, built about eight years after the Federal Savings Bank building, displays similar panels. The unusual pattern of aluminum window *mullions* is evocative of the work of Piet Mondrian, the abstract early twentieth-century Dutch painter.

Like many modernist buildings, it has a flat roof and no projecting *eaves*. The block on the left is composed of stacked, white-glazed brick, fired to achieve a smooth, shiny coating. Stacked brick is a pattern where the *stretchers* are all vertically aligned. This bonding style is structurally weak but appropriate for what is a pure *curtain wall*.

Most citizens don't seem to appreciate this important building. Stop by and show it some love.

# *Part 2*
# BUILDING TYPES

# THE CAPE

*Simplicity is the ultimate sophistication.*
*—Leonardo da Vinci*

We shift now from architectural styles to building types (or house types, in this case). "Architectural style" encompasses the principles, inspiration, composition and detailing embodied in a particular approach to design. "Building type" refers to the building's form, configuration, predominant materials or use. Admittedly, the two concepts do overlap.

The Cape Cod, or "cape," is beloved for its simplicity, durability and adaptability. The cape is a building type, not a style, as it could be clothed in different architectural styles, albeit only a few comfortably.

The prototypical Cape Cod has one and a half stories; a side-facing gable roof (its ridge is thus parallel to the road); a rectangular footprint; a symmetrical façade with five *bays*, including a center entrance; a central chimney; clapboards or shingle siding; and simple *neoclassical* detailing. Early capes often had four rooms on the first floor and two above.

The cape is surprisingly similar to a colonial but with a steep roof accommodating upstairs space, which is necessary given its small footprint. In spite of this parallel, the colonial possesses grandeur, whereas the hallmark of the Cape Cod is its modest, compact form.

# History

The Cape Cod was, of course, named for the coastal area in Massachusetts where it was common in the early years. Shingles were often unpainted, left to weather in the salty air into a rich gray. The cape's low profile made sense in this windswept environment, but the sleeping loft above was dark and cramped. It was reached by a ladder or winding staircase. The exterior was unembellished, yet conservative Yankee craftsmen built a dignity into these simple structures.

The Victorian era brought verticality and more complex building types, so fewer capes were built. It would be unusual, therefore, to see Italianate *brackets* on a cape, though there is one such house on Cocheco Avenue in East Rochester. The Cape Cod reemerged in the 1920s and has endured as one of the most popular house types in the country.

Levitt and Sons was the first builder to produce capes on a large scale. Levittown on Long Island, New York, was developed starting in the late 1940s to serve the expanding suburban housing demand following World War II. The mass production of nearly identical capes became so streamlined that, at its peak, the company could complete a house in just over one day.

There is a collection of three-*bay* capes on Washington Street in Rochester that, like those at Levittown, were probably indistinguishable from one another originally. Over time, though, they have been personalized with dormers, porches, embellished entrances, new windows, new siding and various other modifications. This streetscape is an interesting study in the concept of *variety within unity*.

## PRAY STREET

The cape is a fitting building type to illustrate how a garage can be effectively appended to a house. All too often, the garage is the most conspicuous feature on a dwelling, aggressively jutting forward and obscuring the front door. Planners call this type of dwelling a "snout house." The message is that cars are welcome but human beings are not.

In more polite times, garages were detached structures at the rear or were at least set back beyond the façade of the house. Better yet, they were accessed from a rear alley. If the garage is to be close to the street, it should mimic a carriage house or small barn.

That goal is accomplished in this perfectly composed cape. The garage is a distinct building mass separate from the main house. It is linked by a small section called a *hyphen*. The gable has a steep pitch and has been turned

Pray Street

Sunset Drive

ninety degrees to face the street. There are individual garage doors, instead of the great gaping maw of a double-size door. Garage doors can be made into a design element through the use of a curved top, contrasting color, *transom windows* or beveled corners, as in this example. The element over the doors evokes a hayloft.

## Sunset Drive

This striking red house sits proudly atop a knoll. Many passersby probably assume that it is one of the city's earliest houses.

Sandra Clough and Phillip Guptill strove for authenticity when they built this exceptional reproduction of an early nineteenth-century cape in 1998. The siding is wood clapboard and wood shingle. The windows and exterior storm windows are made of wood. You can tell that it's a contemporary home, however, by the concrete foundation.

The interior features wide pine floors, plaster walls, wood paneling, ceiling beams retrieved from an old barn, seven-and-a-half-foot ceiling heights instead of the customary eight feet and latch doors with vertical boards. In the nineteenth century, the master bedroom was typically the only bedroom with a closet. The owners followed that approach here. Now that is a commitment to authenticity.

# The Colonial

*Listening, not imitation, may be the sincerest form of flattery.*
*—Dr. Joyce Brothers, psychologist and advice columnist*

As mentioned above, the archetypal colonial is like the cape in form except for its full second floor. This is what realtors refer to as a "colonial," whether it was built in 1770, 1880 or 1990.

Sadly, today's standard colonial is graceless. It has no detailing or a deluge of it. The quintessential McMansion erupts with a dizzying collection of dormers, gables and pediments, as if to evoke the village that was eradicated by the explosion of suburbia. The brick and stone veneers look just like that—veneers. The vinyl siding masquerading as wood clapboard is obvious. Some vinyl is now stamped with wood grain, in a more aggressive effort to fool you. Yet grain is not visible through the paint on wood clapboards! The manufacturers were imitating but not listening. As an anonymous wag said, "Style is trendy and fleeting. Bad taste is timeless."

## Crown Point Road and Rockledge Road

It is possible to construct a beautiful colonial without great expense. Dan Begin designed his 2009 Crown Point Road house. Jeff and Kathy DeGrechie designed their 1998 dwelling on Rockledge Road with their builder, Wayne Rowell. The houses could be mistaken for original Georgian and Federal residences, respectively, because they respect traditional principles. Let us examine them in some detail.

Crown Point Road

Rockledge Road

PROPORTIONS. On both houses, there is a satisfying feeling to the pitch of the roof, the ratio of width to height, the restrained size of the windows and the arrangement of the windows.

On the Rockledge house, the spacing next to the center window is slightly greater than the spacing between the outer windows. The upper windows with 6/6 *sashes* are a little shorter than the lower windows with 6/9 *sashes* because the more public nature of the first floor warrants greater ceiling heights. On the Crown Point house, Dan Begin preferred a façade with three *bays*, resulting in a high proportion of wall space, but this is mitigated by the effective spacing of the windows.

SIDING AND TRIM. These houses are made of wood. The *cornerboards*, window *surrounds* and *eaves* have some depth, creating shadows. The clapboards are narrow in width, giving the façade a texture, and on the Crown Point house, Dan uses increasingly narrow boards toward the bottom, creating a rich visual effect. He explained that denser clapboards were sometimes used near the foundation to better withstand the piles of snow.

On both houses, there is decorative trim around the door and, on the Rockledge house, over the windows, but on a well-crafted house, little detailing is actually needed. Outsized, grandiose motifs, like *swan's neck pediments* and corner *quoins*, are liberally tacked onto today's typical colonial. You should strive for beauty through refinement in *proportion* rather than excess, and you will also save money this way.

The Crown Point house features real crown moulding on the *eaves*, which Mr. Begin fabricated himself on a spindle shaper and router table. (Note my highfalutin spelling here, rather than the run-of-the-mill "molding"; I figure this little Britishism is appropriate in homage to Dan's fancy trim work.) I wanted to include some pictures of the handmade guitars that he makes, but I knew you wouldn't buy their being part of the built environment.

WINDOWS. The Rockledge house has wood windows with true divided *lights*, i.e., individual panes of glass attached to individual wood *muntins*. Actually, each *light* is double pane, which provides good insulation.

Admittedly, these are expensive windows, as most true divided *lights* are single rather than double pane. The common alternative is double-pane windows that are not true divided *lights* but rather mimic this look by sandwiching a *muntin* grille between the two full-size panes of glass. A *muntin* grille is one piece resembling a tic-tac-toe cross hatch. These windows are fairly easy to recognize, but at least the internal grille serves to reduce the *scale* of what would otherwise look like a large pane of glass.

Ideally, three *muntin* grilles are employed to better give the impression of real muntins: a metal spacer bar sandwiched between the panes of glass, a grille on the exterior of the *sash* and a grille on the interior of the sash. This is exactly what is done on the Crown Point house.

SHUTTERS. Many new houses display plastic, undersized shutters screwed flat to the wall. If fake shutters are to be used, they should at least be sized properly, to one half the width of the window, as though they were theoretically operable. A far better approach, though, is to eliminate the shutters and embellish the windows with a wide window *surround*, painted a gently contrasting color to that of the main body of the house.

GARAGE. Note that no garage is visible from the front of the houses.

SITE CLEARING. The presence of mature trees around the Rockledge house provides a softening frame for the residence. The DeGrechies hand cleared this area, preserving as many plants as possible, prior to starting construction. Builders often remove all vegetation from a house lot, which makes the construction process more convenient for them but causes erosion, increases landscaping costs and diminishes the character of the property and the neighborhood. (Pay no mind to that grass around Dan's house. I am sure that he has a luxuriant landscaping plan in the works.)

I learned a new term from Jeff DeGrechie. On the standard *hip roof*, the slopes on all four sides are equal. Because Jeff and Kathy wanted more head room on the top floor, the slopes above the shorter sides of the house are steeper than those above the longer sides, resulting in a longer ridge line at the top. This is called a *"bastard hip."* There is your architectural term for the day.

# THE BUNGALOW

*I like the word "indolence." It makes my laziness seem classy.*
*—Bern Williams, writer*

A true bungalow, not the time-share condo that you own at Waterville Valley, is a low-slung one-and-a-half-story house, modest in *scale*, with a generously sized front porch that is integral to the structure. It invites you to just relax.

The bungalow originated in colonial India. The basic dwelling in the eastern province of Bengal, now Bangladesh, was called a "Bangla." It was a small thatched hut with a central living area that led out to a large *veranda*, also an Indian word meaning "generous porch." The British built structures for themselves in India that combined elements of the Bangla with those of the traditional English cottage, later to be called "bungalows."

The bungalow evolved and was the most common house type built in early twentieth-century America. It suited the growing middle class and made it possible for most families to own a home. With its smaller size and simple layout, the bungalow was easy to mass produce, and like the Foursquare, many were purchased by mail order through Sears & Roebuck's and other companies. Cities such as Chicago and Denver have extensive neighborhoods composed entirely of bungalows, offering an exhilarating diversity of this building type. Other contemporary styles, such as English Tudor, Mission, Mediterranean or Colonial Revival, were grafted onto the bungalow, sometimes resulting in a strange eclecticism.

Old Dover Road

The bungalow is a building <u>type</u> and, arguably, an architectural <u>style</u>. It developed in the United States concurrently with the broader Arts and Crafts movement, which was a reaction to the industrialization process, as well as the overly ornate Victorian age. The principles were embodied in the Craftsman style, which emphasized natural materials, respect for local building traditions and fine craftsmanship (which was ironic for a housing type widely built in factories).

## Old Dover Road

This house feels close to the ground because of its long, sheltering roof, overhanging *eaves*, shallow-pitched shed or "cat slide" dormer and X-shaped railings. Construction methods are ostensibly revealed in the exposed rafter ends and triangular braces supporting the overhanging *eaves*.

The Craftsman style (which became virtually synonymous with the "bungalow") emphasized honesty in construction, like modernism, which otherwise propounded a very different philosophy. The ends of horizontal ceiling beams (like the rafter ends) on bungalows often extended beyond the wall. However, like modernism, the Craftsman style often developed its own false aesthetics, with decorative beam ends simply being tacked onto the wall surface.

Constitution Way

## CONSTITUTION WAY

Porches are often supported by squat columns set on high pedestals made of contrasting brick or stone, as demonstrated in this new house. It was built as part of a Planned Unit Development (PUD), an innovative zoning tool that allows a landowner to depart from land-use regulations that are otherwise applicable. In exchange for more flexibility and higher density, the developer must incorporate special features, such as high-quality architecture and landscaping; preservation of open space; and a network of walkable streets, sidewalks, bikeways and other multiuse paths.

## GROVE STREET

Windows are often paired or grouped horizontally to let in more light and ventilation, since the interiors are often dark due to use of natural, dark woods. Bungalows also have these unusual tapered or *battered* porch columns. This pristine, chalet-like house does not have a ground-hugging mien. Rather, one could indeed imagine it high in the White Mountains, perhaps at Waterville Valley.

Both the German word *gemütlich* and the Dutch word *gezellig* translate roughly to "cozy," but they also express domestic warmth, hominess, a cheerful atmosphere in which everyone is welcome and embraced. I think

Grove Street

*gezellig* and *gemütlich* (not a favorite term at the Bauhaus, I am sure) effectively capture the feeling of the bungalow.

The bungalow faded in popularity in the late 1920s and was subsequently considered ugly and ungainly for decades thereafter. Many were torn down. Happily, the bungalow is once again prized for its quality craftsmanship, rich variety and distinct character.

# THE LOG HOUSE

*You cannot build character and courage by taking away man's initiative and independence.*
—*Abraham Lincoln*

The log cabin is imbued with symbolism. We associate it with the virtues of self-sufficiency, humility, honesty and hard work. There has been a resurgence of interest in log houses in recent decades.

The support structure of wood-frame buildings is a skeleton of timbers including posts and beams or wall studs and ceiling joists. Some type of sheathing, such as plywood, is attached to seal up the building. Finally, cladding or siding, like clapboards or shingles, is applied. The logs in a log house, by contrast, constitute the walls in entirety. They support the structure and enclose the space, akin to masonry. Logs also provide an aesthetically suitable wall surface on both the inside and outside, precluding the need for plaster or any exterior finish.

This dwelling type was workable for pioneers to build. At its most elemental, the log cabin was composed of whole tree trunks with the bark intact. It was a rectangle with one room, a dirt floor and no windows. The floor, door and roof were often made of split logs. It is not efficient in its consumption of raw materials, yet a few men working together with an axe and little more could build a basic log cabin in a short time.

English and French settlers in this country did not build log cabins because they were not experienced with the technique. Because the forests of western Europe had been cleared by the late Middle Ages, more efficient

Four Rod
Road

wood-frame methods developed out of necessity. The settlers made primitive shelters of brush and bark until they were able to replicate the post and beam or masonry structures with which they were familiar. German and Scandinavian immigrants, on the other hand, had a log cabin tradition based on still densely forested areas back home.

## Notching and Chinking

The joints at the corners hold the structure together and add complexity and visual interest. The most basic interlocking joint was the saddle or cradle joint. The end of each log was carved out in a curve to hold the next log in the stack. The ends of every log thus extended beyond the corner, past the notch, in that classic overhang. Square notches were more stable but took longer to cut. The most sophisticated structures used a dovetail joint, like the type you see on the inside corners of old drawers.

Logs resting on one another along one side of the cabin do not form a tight seal, even when sawed square. The spaces, or *chinks*, in between had to be filled with chinking, which consisted of dirt, moss, clay, leaves or some type of mortar.

Many companies now produce complete log house kits with choices in house plans, styles, log sizes and notching systems. Generally, each log is precision milled, kiln-dried, precut, predrilled and numbered based on the exact location it is to be placed in the structure. Resistance from the weather is provided not by *chinking* but by tongue-and-groove connections between logs supplemented by rubber or foam gaskets and caulking. The logs are held together with steel spikes, screws or bolts. Consumers, generally, can build the houses themselves or hire the manufacturer or an independent contractor to construct them.

Pine is the most common wood used, although it has to be sealed periodically to protect it from rot, insects and ultraviolet rays. Cedar is considered superior for its resistance to rot. Cypress is also rot resistant but it is used less frequently.

The city assessor's records identify thirty-four log houses in Rochester, with the oldest dating from 1974. The majority of these are clustered in the northwest quadrant of the city. Not surprisingly, most are situated on wooded lots on rural roads. There are six log homes on Four Rod Road.

### Four Rod Road
The handsome structure was built by its owner, James Lamontagne, from a kit in 1976. It is striking for its *gambrel roof*, overhangs at the corners and generously sized porch. The weave of the lattice under the porch provides a foil to the heavy, undressed logs above.

### Bickford Road
Gary and Robynn Jewell built this gem off Walnut Street in 2002. The structure departs significantly from the traditional log house with its dramatic roof lines and expanses of glass. The Jewells enjoy fine views of Blue Job Mountain from their front deck.

Note the nine *purlins* under the overhanging metal roof. Most pitched roofs are supported by rafters, which run with the slope from *eave* to ridge. Purlins, in contrast, extend horizontally from gable wall to gable wall. For a roof

Bickford Road

composed of heavy timbers, as on early log cabins, each gable wall provides better support than the ridge beam.

The emergence of contemporary log houses is a good thing. A traditional building form has been revived, sustainable natural materials are being used in abundance, technology is expanding upon revered old methods and we are seeing a renewed commitment to good design, quality craftsmanship and beauty.

# THE DUPLEX

*A joy that is shared is a joy made double.*
*—English proverb*

Many duplexes, or "two-family houses," are asymmetrical, with one unit on the first floor and another on the second and third floors, often with a *gambrel* roof. There are blocks and blocks of these houses in the older suburbs west of Boston, in Cambridge, Arlington, Somerville and Medford. However, it is the plethora of side-by-side, symmetrical duplexes in Rochester, also called "double houses," that catch one's attention with their charming matching halves.

## Mixed Use

The duplexes in Rochester are not clustered but rather are interspersed throughout older single-family areas. They blend in and add variety to their neighborhoods. Duplexes would generally not be well received within our new single-family subdivisions. Today, most development across the country is aggressively segregated by use: single family in one area, multifamily in another and commercial relegated to the highway.

People want to live with others just like themselves and to have predictable, homogeneous, if utterly bland environments, or so it would seem. Many zoning ordinances even separate single-family areas from one another by minimum lot sizes with the silliest increments—half-acre homes here,

Cocheco Avenue

three-quarter-acre homes there—so that, heaven forefend, there shall be no intermingling of the classes.

In years past, our neighborhoods embodied diversity through a fine-grained mix of uses. Different housing types, small stores and even workplaces were located close to one another. There was a synergy in having these various activities close by. Andres Duany compares the contemporary city with an uncooked omelet: it is like eating each of the ingredients separately. This is not to say that in a traditional neighborhood any type of structure could be erected next to any other. For the most part, we somehow naturally knew how to combine things harmoniously.

The separation of uses, spread-out nature of development on bigger lots and concentration of traffic onto fewer, large-*scale* arteries requires us to drive for virtually all of our daily activities. In contrast, a dense network of streets, like a modified grid, allows for a richer, more interesting pattern of development, and one friendly to pedestrians who have many alternate routes to follow. Life on a cul-de-sac is serviceable for small children, for whom riding a tricycle round and round is satisfying. However, older children want to explore the wider world, and the streets beyond the cul-de-sac are often dangerous for walking or riding.

# Affordable Housing

For a long-established, urban community, Rochester has surprisingly few examples of other traditional multifamily building types, such as the asymmetrical duplexes, small apartment buildings, triple deckers or row houses, which are really extended versions of the side-by-side duplex. In the neighborhoods ringing downtown Rochester, East Rochester and Gonic, the nineteenth- and early twentieth-century millworkers were housed in rather closely packed and modestly *scaled*, but nicely articulated, single- and two-family houses.

The time-honored development patterns provided affordable housing organically. It was not necessary to build large-*scale*, isolated projects. Students, senior citizens and lower-income families could live in smaller houses on smaller lots, row houses, multifamily dwellings, accessory units above garages and apartments over stores, all integrated into the neighborhood in a pleasing and mutually beneficial way.

The side-by-side duplex is surprisingly versatile for housing because it can provide two rental units as an investment; it can provide one rental unit for an owner-occupant and help pay the mortgage; it can be a condominium, also called a "condex," where each party owns an interior unit but the shell of the building and underlying land is owned jointly; or it can be arranged "fee

Pickering Road

87

simple," like some town houses, where each party owns one entire vertical half of the building, from foundation to roof, including the land underneath, which is divided into two lots.

## COCHECO AVENUE

Duplexes do not require elaborate ornamentation to be attractive structures, as the symmetry is innately satisfying. Good proportions, good materials and some minimal adornment are all that is needed. The pair of two-story *bays* lends some distinction to this dwelling.

## PICKERING ROAD

This house turns the steep gable to face the street. Shifting the entrances to the wider side of the house allows for a more gracious central hall for each unit. Those voluptuous *bay windows*, paired *brackets* at the *cornices*, fish scale shingles and half gables at the side entries give the house character. Older single-family areas—those with class—would surely welcome this house in their neighborhoods.

# DOWNTOWN BUILDINGS

*Oh, a day in the city square, there is no such pleasure in life!*
*—Robert Browning*

R esidents savor reminiscing about old Rochester, especially the downtown and its long disappeared businesses and personalities.

An article entitled "1914 Rochester Today with Glimpses of its Past" by Adeline Estes Wright testified to the vibrancy of the downtown at that time and particularly of Hanson Street:

> *Almost every kind of business and profession is to be found on this street: livery stable, blacksmith shop, restaurants, provision market, florist, undertaking rooms, bakeries, barber, tailor, harness shops, hardware, furniture, clothing, dry goods, millinery, music and stationery, grocery and fruit stores, pool and billiard rooms, dye house, boot and shoe blacking rooms, photographer's studio, real estate, dentist, doctor and lawyer's offices, and the rooms occupied by the Hanson's American Band.*\*

This is remarkable given that Hanson Street is only one block long!

Hanson Street was built in 1849 as a private street by Dominicus Hanson, who leased adjacent land for buildings. In 1901, he laid the street with fifty-six thousand granite blocks. Hanson Street was subsequently conveyed to the city, which in 1949 placed asphalt over the blocks. Many of these squares were felicitously reused, though, as part of recent renovations of the street.

---

\* http://www.geocities.com/powerofz7/1914.html.

North Main Street-1

Prior to World War II, most residents of Rochester lived in compact neighborhoods adjacent to the downtown, or in the outlying villages of East Rochester and Gonic, and walked to meet their daily needs. Striding in the open air with neighbors and fellow citizens reinforced a sense of community.

One of the most beloved figures in recent history was Willis "Red" Hayes, a police officer who directed traffic in Central Square for decades before automatic controls were installed. He had red hair and gestured flamboyantly as he worked the intersection. Red, an emissary of good cheer for the downtown, died in 1986.

Coming downtown was not only convenient and welcoming, but it was also aesthetically rewarding. The traditional Main Street is relatively narrow, with two- or three-story buildings on each side, creating a satisfying sense of space. There are no front setbacks and no side setbacks, so the buildings work together to form a "streetwall," as shown in the three photographs in this section. Contrast this arrangement with the commercial strip, which provides no spatial definition. The road is extra wide with squat buildings placed far away, beyond a great expanse of parking.

# Challenges for Downtowns

Most downtowns are the geographic, historic, governmental, commercial and cultural centers of their communities. Yet they face numerous challenges today: people drive to shopping and other destinations and seek easy parking; businesses prefer the simplicity of new, one-story structures; national chains require larger building footprints that do not fit into smaller buildings on tighter lots; and zoning, building, fire and disability codes make it expensive or even impossible to retrofit older, multistory buildings or build suitable new ones.

Rochester's esteemed Main Street program, sponsored by the National Trust for Historic Preservation, is working to revitalize the central business district. Main Street followed the acronym DOPE: Design—enhancing storefronts, creating agreeable outdoor spaces and preserving architecture; Organization—getting the downtown merchants and property owners to coordinate their efforts; Promotion—advertising the downtown and holding special events to draw the public; and Economic restructuring—rebalancing the mix of businesses and providing training for merchants. It is a simple but brilliant formula, though I believe that Main Street has, understandably, dropped this particular acronym.

North Main Street-2

If for no other reason, we should keep our downtown vital so that we can experience the extraordinary architecture showcased there.

### North Main Street-1
This one-block-long section of North Main Street, between Wakefield and Union Streets, is the center of Rochester's downtown. It is also, not coincidentally, the place with the strongest sense of enclosure. The Hayes Block on the left, built circa 1878, housed an opera house on the upper two floors. The circa 1900 Salinger Block on the right features an exceptional glazed white-brick façade, individual treatment of each of the four stories, beautiful arched windows and floral sandstone trim.

### North Main Street-2
The Hartigan Block on the left, built circa 1901, is distinctive for the three pairs of round-headed windows in the third floor, nicely echoed by arched *eyebrows* over each pair and the arcading pattern, i.e., the series of arches, in the brickwork above. The *hoods* over the second-floor windows are just slightly rounded.

The Elm Block on the right, circa 1900, is asymmetrical, with greater spacing among the four windows on the right half of the façade. This is not particularly noticeable, but it is oddly engaging. The decorative brickwork is

South Main Street

delicately rendered with a checkerboard band over the second-floor windows, a saw-tooth pattern over the third-floor windows and *corbelling* in the *cornice*.

## SOUTH MAIN STREET

The structure on the left has a fine *bowfront*. The *neoclassical*-style brick building in the middle is the Chamber of Commerce, thankfully still situated right in the heart of the downtown.

The former Norway Plains Savings Bank, built in 1903, resembles a Roman temple. The four free-standing two-story columns are *fluted* and topped with *Corinthian capitals*. The building is made of smooth limestone blocks resting on a polished granite base. Note the slight asymmetry. This is the city's most monumental building, projecting permanence and probity, fitting qualities for a bank.

# GOVERNMENT BUILDINGS

*Twentieth-century America has seen a steady, persistent decline in the visual and emotional power of its public buildings, and this has been accompanied by a not less persistent decline in the authority of public order.*
—*Daniel Patrick Moynihan, former United States senator*

The enduring, pernicious effects of modernism are especially evident in the poor quality of government buildings erected in the past half century. Architects today seem embarrassed to use elements like the arches and *quoins*, which are unmistakable elements on these three buildings. So instead, we get blank brick walls.

Rochester was prosperous in the early decades of the twentieth century. One write-up in 1914 referred to it as a modern city with "broad, shaded streets, handsome residences, an unlimited supply of pure water, scientific sanitation, electric lights, superior railroad and electric car facilities, fine schools and good churches." The community's pride was reflected in the high-quality government buildings erected at the time.

## SOUTH MAIN STREET

The Rochester Public Library was built in 1905. The city's postmaster had written Andrew Carnegie in New York City asking for a contribution for a new library. He stated that the town was originally settled, in part, by Scottish immigrants, which was true, but probably not necessary to sway Mr. Carnegie. Carnegie sent a check for $20,000 (equivalent to about $500,000 today) with his customary stipulation that the town provide the land and at least $2,000 annually for maintenance.

South Main Street

Andrew Carnegie (1835–1919) was a poor child when his family emigrated from Scotland. He amassed an estimated $500 million in the steel industry. Carnegie later dedicated himself to philanthropy, funding over 1,700 free municipal libraries in the United States and 800 libraries in other English-speaking countries. Each of the Carnegie libraries I have seen in pictures is unique. What a magnificent legacy!

This is what a library should look like. The elevated central *pavilion* gives the building a noble presence. It has a profusion of blonde-colored corner *quoins*, contrasting with the red brick. Matching pairs of *monolithic* granite columns rest on tall pedestals that flank the entry. A pair of reclining lions on the *cheek blocks* would complete the composition.

The first librarian here was the redoubtable Lillian Parshley, who served for forty years, until her death in 1945. I am told that she ran a tight ship. In the early years, the library had closed stacks; you had to request a book, which the staff would then retrieve. If Ms. Parshley did not think a particular book was appropriate for you, she would simply not get it.

The library housed a museum that, like many municipal museums, had a collection of eccentric objects. There was a dried puffer fish, an Edison phonograph, moccasins purportedly worn by Sitting Bull and a meteorite. When the library ran out of space, the objects were given to the Rochester Historical Society or Dover's Woodman Institute or sold at auction.

## WAKEFIELD STREET

I think that Rochester City Hall is the city's most outstanding building. It is noteworthy that the architect, George Gilman Adams, had no formal architectural education.

There is much to admire in this 1908 *neoclassical* structure. It has a full, pleasing mass and a prominent entry. The wall surfaces are richly textured with a *rusticated* brick pattern on the first floor. The building has strong horizontal definition with its stone foundation, three main levels of varying heights separated by *belt courses* and fine *cornice*. It has a strong vertical character exemplified in the corner *quoins*, tall windows and central *pavilion*.

Wakefield Street

City hall has a variety of window treatments, including flat-headed first-floor windows with *sidelights* and stained-glass *transoms*, tall arched windows and squat windows in the attic, each with a different window *surround*. A *cartouche*, set within a *broken* arch above the city hall sign, crowns the composition. A *cartouche* is an ornamental scroll, circle or oval, often bearing an inscription. The term also refers to jewelry, so watch for opportunities to declare, "I simply adore your cartouche!"

## NORTH MAIN STREET

The federal government erected this post office building in 1913. The post office relocated to Allen Street, and the building is now the Rochester District Courthouse. It is Rochester's only example of the stately Beaux-Arts style. This style is named for the Ecole des Beaux-Arts, i.e., School of Fine Arts, in Paris, where many American architects studied at the end of the nineteenth century.

Beaux-Arts is the most monumental architectural style. It was used for important public buildings such as train stations, art museums and libraries, particularly in cities like New York, Chicago and Washington, D.C. Beaux-Arts structures were built of marble, granite or limestone, but also of brick, which doesn't convey the same grandeur.

North Main Street

The design is effusive, epitomizing the nineteenth-century French feeling of *horror vacui*, which means dread of unadorned wall surfaces. Examine the creative use of *headers* and *stretchers* and different-colored brick to make wonderful patterns. Unfortunately, the use of muted colors of brick and limestone obscures the images. I suspect that the federal government may have instructed the architect to tone it down a little.

Imagine sculpted figures of the Roman gods—Jupiter, Juno, Mars, Mercury, Neptune and Venus—standing on those pedestals above the parapet wall. That would be grand.

# Schools

*We shape our buildings; thereafter they shape us.*
*—Winston Churchill*

Nowhere is this statement more applicable than in our schools, all too many of which resemble massive, formless crates, again in fealty to the credo of modernism (or due to plain stinginess).

Most older schools were handsome, multistory red brick structures, reflecting a civic pride. What message does the Spaulding High School building convey to its occupants? It announces that they are valued members of the community and that they are engaged in something important.

## Neighborhood Schools

The size and location of schools also contribute to the message. Rochester has eight elementary schools, and each is a neighborhood-based school. The middle school and high school are located in accessible core areas.

The National Trust for Historic Preservation published "Why Johnny Can't Walk to School; Historic Neighborhood Schools in the Age of Sprawl." The report argues that local schools serve as anchors for the community, provide resources for the immediate area and enhance public health by allowing children to walk and ride bicycles to school.

There are obstacles to renovation. General building codes are oriented primarily toward new construction, and when applied rigidly to existing buildings, rehabilitation becomes unduly expensive. Some educators prefer outsized schools due to economies of scale: they can offer more subjects, bigger ball fields and more competitive sports teams. However, the National Trust report states that such facilities "shroud young people in a cloak of anonymity." It adds that "smaller schools produce better academic results, lower dropout rates, and less school violence."*

Walking or biking to school and home again instills a sense of valuable independence in young people. To be sure, if we build large-*scale* institutions on former farm fields we will need the extensive amount of acreage required by state standards to accommodate huge parking lots, since students will now need to drive to get there.

## WAKEFIELD STREET-1

The munificent Spaulding family paid for the construction of Spaulding High School. The school opened in 1939, the year World War II started, and there are bomb shelters in the basement. This is the community's signature building, along with Rochester City Hall. It is rendered in the Georgian Revival style, influenced by Harvard University's river houses in Cambridge, Massachusetts. The inspiration for the high school's two green-domed *cupolas* was likely Harvard's elegant 1930 Eliot House.

The two wings are dignified in form with their red brick, slate *hip roof*, two tiers of 12/12 windows, nice 3-8-3 rhythm in the *bays* and widely spaced dormers. Notwithstanding the school's architectural link with Harvard, the central section and clock *tower* unmistakably resemble a traditional New England church or meetinghouse. It is almost perfect, but, unfortunately, I doubt that the school district would entertain adding a *spire*.

This main block is nicely integrated with the wings in its colors and materials. However, it stands apart from them with its forward placement, higher *eave* level and rich embellishments, not the least of which are, yes, its *arches* and *quoins*. The middle two columns in the porch are spaced slightly wider, visually framing the three-stage *tower* and accommodating the properly proportioned *Palladian window* between them. These are certainly Rochester's finest *Corinthian* columns. Here is the architectural term for the day: *pargeting*. It refers to that graceful ornamental plasterwork in the *pediment*.

---

* Constance E. Beaumont and Elizabeth G. Pianca, "Why Johnny Can't Walk to School: Historic Neighborhood Schools in the Age of Sprawl," National Trust for Historic Preservation (October 2002).

Wakefield Street-1

## WAKEFIELD STREET-2

Surely, there was much angst in 1975 when students were relocated from this cherished building to the city's most unloved edifice. The Community Center, rendered in what we may call the Soviet Brutalist style, was the high school for sixteen years. A rare beauty indeed.

## COCHECO AVENUE

The Nancy Loud School is the only wood-frame school, and the oldest school in the district, built in 1880. It was renamed in 2008 for its beloved principal, who retired after decades of service. When I spoke with Nancy, we agreed that the district was wise to include her full name in the dedication, lest the children try to live up to the moniker "The Loud School."

It is a charming building and one that I would feel content having my child walk to each morning. It has a curious mix of elements: an L-shaped structure enveloping a lower section (like a mama lion embracing its cub), narrow clapboards and perfectly *proportioned* windows that provide a fine texture, two forlorn *Palladian window* motifs and that *tower* getting ready to take off!

Railroad Avenue

## School Street

This is the School Street School located on School Street. We should rename the street in tribute to the school: School Street School Street.

In spite of its droll name, this is one poker-faced building, reminiscent of Foursquare style. The massive brick block is mitigated, though, by the *belt courses* breaking it into horizontal sections, the delicate white *brackets* supporting the *cornice* and those sly dormers.

## Railroad Avenue

The Gonic School building, constructed in 1897, projects rectitude. You feel like the structure itself will see through your kid's malarkey. Understandably, the school district matched the original as closely as possible for the 1987 addition (not shown).

*Opposite, top*: Wakefield Street-2
*Opposite, middle*: Cocheco Avenue
*Opposite, bottom*: School Street

# CHURCHES

*When I lately stood with a friend before* [the cathedral of] *Amiens…he asked me how it happens that we can no longer build such piles? I replied: "Dear Alphonse, men in those days had convictions, we moderns have opinions and it requires something more than an opinion to build a Gothic cathedral."*
—Heinrich Heine, German romantic poet

Much of the history of architecture is the history of religious architecture. In the Western World, this is the story of temples in ancient Egypt, Greece and Rome and churches from that point on. We may give disproportionate attention to these buildings, though, because they were prominent, plus they were built of durable materials and lasted, where other buildings crumbled.

New England has an extraordinary repository of iconic Colonial and Post-Colonial period meetinghouses, as churches in this period were generally called. Religious services and town meetings were often held there, and until the Revolution, church and state were largely merged. Massachusetts, for instance, had a state church until 1826, and membership was a prerequisite for voting.

The meetinghouse was at the center of the community, often situated alongside the archetypical New England town green. It was part of an ensemble that might have included a burial ground, a town hall, an inn and tavern, a country store and a handsome collection of white houses. There were likely trade shops nearby, and in earlier times, the stocks and whipping post were often located close to the meetinghouse.

South Main Street-1

# Meetinghouse Design

London suffered a devastating fire in 1666. In the aftermath, the renowned architect Christopher Wren designed numerous churches in the heart of the city. His buildings and those of other British architects of the Baroque era, i.e., the seventeenth and early eighteenth centuries, were the inspiration (direct or indirect) for many of New England's meetinghouses. These meetinghouses are a wonderful example of *variety within unity*. They are *neoclassical* in design, having been built in Georgian, Federal or Greek Revival styles. Later Italianate-style churches, such as the First United Methodist Church (below), continued the basic form. While the designs were simple, they achieved a rare elegance, partly due to the refinement of the form over time.

The structures are almost universally symmetrical. They have a front-facing gable, even on Georgian and Federal buildings, with a center entrance or perhaps several entry doors. A graceful *portico* might be surmounted by a *Palladian window* or a *lunette*. One of the more enchanting elements is the green or black shutters that enclose semicircular windows. They are unmistakable, when unlatched, with their flanking, wing-like quarter-round tops.

Meetinghouses were customarily built of wood and painted white, both on the exterior and interior, partly as a symbol of religious purity. They were simple in form and ornamentation, due to limited funds and a humility, rooted in Puritanism. Windows were clear glass; stained glass did not emerge until the advent of the Gothic Revival.

The most noteworthy feature of the New England meetinghouse is the *tower*. It is useful to clarify a few terms, the better for you to quiz and confound your fellow parishioners. A church *tower* is the base structure, almost always square in plan. A *spire* is a tall, tapering conical or *pyramidal* element. It may commence at the roof or from a tower, in which case, the entire element is a steeple (tower + spire = steeple). A *cupola* is an ornamental structure, often with a domed roof. The *belfry* contains a bell and is open to the air or screened with *louvers*, a frame with fixed or movable slats.

The most elaborate steeples have several stages, and many have bells cast in Paul Revere's Boston foundry. The steeple at Park Street Church in Boston, with its delicately telescoping stages, is the most beautiful that I have seen.

South Main Street-2

# Church Interiors

The meetinghouse was typically a simple rectangle, often with a *vestibule* at the entrance. It had a central aisle and sometimes side aisles and second-floor galleries supported by columns. Unmarried men and women were often separated: "bachelors" sat in one gallery and "maids and spinsters" in another.

The most lavish features were typically a brass and crystal chandelier and the high pulpit flanked by curved stairways. The best pews were often reserved for those who contributed most to the church. More affluent churches built box pews that retained heat better, offered some privacy and allowed families to add personal upholstering.

Many churches did not have any heat until the early 1800s, when a stove might be installed in the front. Older parishioners often brought foot stoves filled with coals. Some would bring puppies to keep on their laps. As an amusing side note, in the 1600s, a deacon would circulate holding a stick with a feather on one end and a stone wrapped in leather on the other. A lady dozing would get tickled under the chin; her snoring male counterpart would get rapped on the head.

# Gothic Revival

The imposing Trinity Church in New York City was completed in 1846. It was one of the first examples of Gothic Revival in *ecclesiastical* architecture in the country and ushered in the style as the predominant fashion for churches. Gothic Revival's emphatic verticality is a fitting metaphor for reaching toward heaven.

Gothic architecture had nothing to do with the Goths. This Germanic tribe invaded Rome in the fifth century and the style was developed seven hundred years later, in the twelfth century and beyond. Italian Renaissance artists, looking back on the style, thought it so crude that it could have been developed by the Goths.

### South Main Street-1
The Congregational church is the descendant of the first church in Rochester. The original meetinghouse led by Parson Main, built in 1730 on Haven Hill, was the center of the fledgling community. The building was moved to the Common years later and subsequently moved again to its present location, where, in 1867, it was remodeled and enlarged. The fine steeple rises in four stages, culminating in an octagonal *spire*.

### South Main Street-2
The 1868 First United Methodist and the Congregational church, above, form a gateway for those entering the city from the south, and their steeples punctuate the view from various vantage points around the city (you know, from each of our seven hills). The Methodist church *tower terminates the vista* nicely as one drives south on North Main Street.

This is an exceptional example of Italianate church architecture with its copious rounded features: its small *rose window*; elongated, round-headed windows; large, arched doorway; *arcaded corbelling*; and arches in the tower. The clock is owned and maintained by city hall.

Main Street, East Rochester

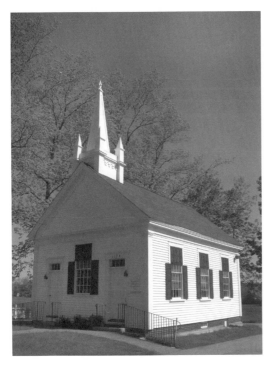

Salmon Falls Road

There is a treasure inside. The pipe organ has about one thousand pipes, ranging in size from eight feet in height to one the size of a fountain pen. The façade for the organ pipes, adorned in gold leaf stenciling, is gorgeous.

## MAIN STREET, EAST ROCHESTER
The 1873 Bethany United Methodist Church is one of Rochester's few historic churches with Gothic features: a *pointed arch* window and two steeply pitched openings in the *belfry*. Otherwise, this eclectic structure is rendered in the *neoclassical* mode, including the 1908 entry porch. The four-staged steeple, added about 1888, is a powerful element.

## SALMON FALLS ROAD
Walnut Grove Baptist Church was erected in the same year as the Methodist church. It was named for nearby Walnut Grove Farm, which actually had hickory trees, whose nuts resemble walnuts, rather than walnut trees. It is lovely to drive along lower Salmon Falls Road, past the rolling fields, connected barns and meandering river, past this charming country church.

# MILLS

*The beautiful is as useful as the useful…and perhaps more so.*
—*Victor Hugo*

Imagine—or remember—what a different place Rochester was half a century ago. Shoe and textile mills were humming throughout the city. Men and women worked as weavers, winders, spinners, stitchers, carders, dressers and dyers…not to mention yarn weighers, spool strippers and roving carriers.

By 1806, industrialization was underway in Rochester with six tanneries, two gristmills, a sawmill and a fulling mill (fulling increases the weight of wool by shrinking and beating it). The population surged between 1840 and 1860, when people left the farms and immigrants poured in to work in the expanding woolen mills. Rail reached the city in 1849. More people moved here from 1870 to 1880, when the shoe mills became well established. Most of the mills tapped water power from the Cocheco River in downtown Rochester and Gonic and the Salmon Falls River in East Rochester.

## Shoe Manufacturing

By the final third of the nineteenth century, most parts of the shoemaking process had been automated. One of the few remaining procedures requiring hand labor was shaping the shoe around the last and sewing it together. The last is a block shaped like a foot. A skilled craftsman could last 50 pairs of

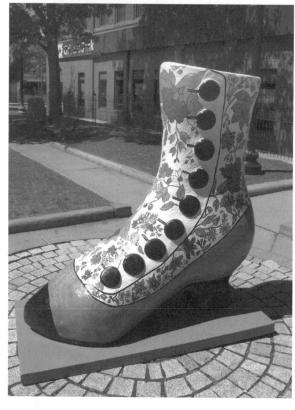

*Above*: Pickering Road

*Left*: Wakefield Street

shoes per day. In 1874, an immigrant in Lynn, Massachusetts, another shoe capital, invented a mechanical laster that revolutionized the industry. This machine could last upward of 750 shoes per day. New England then became the center of the shoe industry in the United States.[*]

Twin brothers Edwin and Ebenezer Wallace were in the tanning business. They decided to use some of their extra leather to make boots and founded the Wallace Shoe Company in 1854. This move proved propitious when the Civil War started seven years later. Their factory, which was located on the present Walgreen's site, was at one time the largest shoe manufacturer in New Hampshire. They were also the city's biggest employer, with over seven hundred workers in 1901.

Colby Footwear in Gonic was one of the few ladies' shoe manufacturers that made footwear up to a size fourteen. How many women do you know with feet that big? Evidently, the shoes were also solidly constructed. From about 1985 to 1995, according to Don Silberstein, who was vice-president at the time, Colby's products were popular with a particular underserved clientele: large transvestites. (According to Mr. Silberstein, this was a very small part of their business and not one that the company actually courted.)

The shoe industry declined through much of the twentieth century. The former Wallace building was home to Al-Gor [sic] Shoe Company in the 1980s. Guess which presidential candidate posed for a photograph in front in 1988.

Sadly, due to automation and lower wage schedules in the South and overseas, shoe manufacturing jobs are all gone. Colby Footwear, the city's last shoemaker, closed in 2000.

The Roman architect Vitruvius stated in *De Architectura*, his treatise on architecture, that buildings should have "Commodity, Firmness, and Delight." This means that the structure should be useful, physically sturdy and beautiful. Although aesthetic considerations were not a priority of their owners, New England mill buildings epitomize those qualities.

### PICKERING ROAD

The Gonic Manufacturing Company, which made woolen goods, was the largest employer in Gonic. Its founder, Nicholas Whitehouse, lived in the fabulous house at the head of Gonic Square (see "Italianate").

The façade of the Gonic Mill brings to mind the mammoth complexes on the Merrimack River in Manchester, Lowell and Lawrence. The main tenant in this former mill, Brand Partners, did an excellent job preserving

---

[*] Fowler, "The Shoemaking History of Rochester."

and showcasing the wood beams and columns, iron tie-rod trusses and decorative brickwork on the interior.

## Wakefield Street

In recognition of Rochester's shoe history, Art Esprit, a local nonprofit arts organization, created sculptures of eleven different shoes. They went on temporary display in various outdoor downtown locations in 2009. This is a depiction of a lady's boot style popular around 1800.

## North Main Street

Norway Plains Company erected the building with the *belfry* in 1846. This entity produced more wool blankets for the Union army during the Civil War than any other company. Wyandotte Worsted Company, the last mill at this site, closed in 1972.

The buildings were vacant for many years, and the city government acquired the property through tax liens. Demolition was contemplated. The complex, fortunately, was conveyed to the Rochester Housing Authority, which renovated it into seventy-two one-bedroom units for the elderly and handicapped. Wyandotte Falls housing development opened in 1986.

Go to the patio behind the building and you will see water racing through a sluiceway under the structure. This runs an electricity-generating turbine. The housing authority granted a one-hundred-year lease to a company from Laconia that operates the system and sells the electricity to the Public Service Company of New Hampshire. Water power lives!

## Old Dover Road

I'm cheating here. The Merchants Plaza building was not a mill, but it had an industrial-type use: as a trolley barn. A trolley line started at this building, ran down Old Dover Road and terminated at a similar building, now Riverside Garage, on High Street in Somersworth.

This structure recalls church architecture with the tall nave-like (i.e., referring to the main aisle in a church) central block and lower sections akin to side aisles. Note the unusual *clerestory windows* along the top of the central section, and step inside also to see the fine metal truss work.

Jean Twombly told me that her father, Edward Rumazza, bought the building some time after the trolley barn shut down and hosted ballroom dancing, semiprofessional basketball and boxing there. At the start of World War II, Mr. Rumazza laid down maple flooring and converted the space to the Humoresque Roller Skating Rink. It was named for one of Jean's mother's

North Main Street

Old Dover Road

favorite songs written by the great Czech composer Antonin Dvorak. The rink closed in 1982, after forty-three years. Nearly three decades later, many people still refer to the building as "The Humoresque."

Word is that Jim McManus, police commissioner and longtime city council member, was a pretty good roller skater in his day. (This comes not from Jim but from another source.) He worked his way up at the Humoresque from "bottle boy," picking up stray bottles of Jic-Jac Tonic, to "skate boy," handing out skates to customers to clamp onto their street shoes. You had to pay extra for actual boot skates. Finally, he was promoted to "floor boy," a coveted position. He was the guy zipping around with the whistle making sure you behaved. Jim could train a new cadre of cops on skates, armed with whistles, to patrol the downtown.

# BARNS

*You can make a small fortune in farming...provided you start with a large one.*
*—anonymous*

We lament the passage of the agrarian way of life. Large-scale factory farming, refrigerated trucking and the encroachment of new development has pushed much agriculture out of the region and led to the introduction of what author James Howard Kunstler calls "the 3,000-mile Caesar salad." Farming in New Hampshire is not as prevalent as it once was, but it still has a distinct presence.

New Hampshire agriculture produces approximately $1 billion worth of goods annually, accounting for about 2 percent of the state's economy. Nearly half a million acres of land are farmed, accounting for about 8 percent of the state's total land area. New Hampshire has several important programs for preserving farming, open space and agricultural structures. Current use law boosts the affordability of farming by taxing undeveloped land based upon its actual use rather than its potential development value. The Land and Community Heritage Investment Program provides matching grants to municipalities and nonprofit organizations to preserve important natural and cultural resources.

## Agricultural Structures

New Hampshire's Barn Preservation Act provides for a reduced local property assessment to be set somewhere between 25 percent and 75

Salmon Falls Road

percent of the full value if the owner grants a preservation easement committing to maintaining the structure while the lower assessment is in effect.

The law covers a wide range of agricultural structures: silos, sawmills, gristmills, icehouses, cider houses, windmill houses, granaries, creameries, poultry coops, piggeries, blacksmith shops, farrier shops (where horses receive shoes or medical treatment), hop houses (for drying, bleaching and preserving hops for beer) and corncribs (structures with slatted sides allowing air to circulate and dry the picked corn). Regrettably, there are few of these artifacts remaining in Rochester.

We do have one particularly interesting contemporary agricultural structure. In 1980, Bud Meader built a sugarhouse out of logs. It is visible from Meaderboro Road on the right side of the Meader compound. Bud explained that forty gallons of sap will boil down to only one gallon of syrup. Because the sap needs to boil continuously for almost a month and has to be watched constantly, sugarhouses usually have sleeping bunks. Bud's family has been producing maple syrup or maple sugar, which is simply boiled longer than syrup, since 1769.

The most evocative agricultural structure is, of course, the barn. Eric Sloane, author of *An Age of Barns*, describes walking one night into an abandoned barn that he had recently purchased: "At once, I seemed to have an overwhelming sense of satisfaction and safeness: there was a welcome softness of hay underfoot, and although they could not be seen, the surrounding walls and the oversize beams made themselves felt, almost like something alive there in the darkness. The incense of seasoned wood and the perfume of dry hay mingled to create that distinctive fragrance which only an ancient barn possesses."*

# Connected Barns

Since arriving in Rochester, I have marveled at its many connected barns. These linked structures allowed a farmer to tend his animals during the cold months without having to go outside. This building form is largely peculiar to the four northern New England states, with a large concentration in eastern New Hampshire.

A typical connected barn goes something like this: the house in the front is connected to a rear ell, which is connected to the woodshed, which is connected to the carriage shed, which is connected to the outhouse, which is connected to the barn. These structures were sometimes built all at once and sometimes incrementally over time. In the 1600s, some towns considered connected barns fire hazards and banned them.

Portland Street

---

* Sloane, *An Age of Barns*, 9.

Lowell Street

## SALMON FALLS ROAD

There are numerous fine connected barns along Salmon Falls Road still surrounded by extensive acreage. Note the unusual *fenestration*, *cupola* with concave roof and fine overall *proportions* of this fantastic barn.

## PORTLAND STREET

There are a number of connected barns on Portland Street but on much smaller lots than those on Salmon Falls Road. These were smaller farmsteads or owned by families who did not farm, but rather needed a barn in which to maintain their horse and carriage.

## LOWELL STREET

You might have wondered about this unusual barn-type building in the woods visible from Lowell Street. It is a work and storage area for Steve Plante, who lives behind it. There are some great details: the banks of horizontal windows like those on horse barns, the double sloped roof, the corner entryway with a single *colonette*, the *lunette* and the hoist and pulley used to lift material into the loft. There is a custom-made weather vane of three winged pigs atop the *cupola* (difficult to see in the photograph). The Plante's daughter, Jessica, who was twelve when the barn was built in 1997, fancied this chimerical image.

# THE MANSIONS OF
# WAKEFIELD STREET

*True wealth is not measured in money or status or power. It is measured in the*
*legacy we leave behind for those we love and those we inspire.*
—*Cesar Chavez*

We now look at three superb buildings, all situated along one short section of Wakefield Street. One hundred years ago, people proclaimed their wealth with large houses situated on fine streets. They were prominently located for all to see. There were strong class distinctions, but the rich dwelt among us. A workingman might pass a mill owner strolling on Wakefield Street in the evening. Those with large fortunes today tend to seek exclusivity, living on enormous, private tracts of land, often behind gates. Yet, ironically, we have a greater sense of equality now. These changed circumstances may account for the diminished sense of noblesse oblige expressed today.

## The Spauldings

Jonas Spaulding started Spaulding Fiber Company. He developed a special material made from recycled scraps of leather from the local shoe industry. This "shoeboard" was used for shoe heels and products such as lunchboxes, violin cases and speaker horns on early radios. Both of his sons, Huntley and Rolland, were involved in this and other businesses. Rochester's Spaulding Composites Company descended from the firm.

*Left*: Wakefield Street-1

*Below*: Wakefield Street-1

Rolland Spaulding served as governor from 1915 to 1917 and Huntley, a decade later, from 1927 to 1929. Rochester was also home to a third governor, Samuel Felker, whose term ran from 1913 to 1915.

Rolland Spaulding had one daughter, Virginia. She married Bill Champlin, whose family was in the timber business and operated Champlin Box Factory. Virginia Champlin shared her family's philanthropic ethic. She bequeathed her house on Rochester Hill Road and surrounding acreage to the Homemakers of Strafford County. Mrs. Champlin was president of the local garden club and was responsible for the spectacular lilacs planted along Route 108. Incidentally, both Rochester, New Hampshire, and Rochester, New York (the author's hometown), are known as "the Lilac City."

Dr. Peter Ejarque, a cardiologist, conducted his medical practice in the Huntley building for about twenty-five years. When he retired, Dr. Ejarque planned to sell the property, but his sons convinced him that the building would make a good bed-and-breakfast. The Governor's Inn opened on May 19, 1992. The Ejarque family later purchased the Rolland Estate next door from the law firm of Cooper, Hall, Whittum, and Shillaber in January 2000. The carriage house of the Rolland Estate was inaugurated as the Café at the Governor's Inn in May 2002. A new establishment in the Huntley called Spaulding Steak and Ale recently opened.

### WAKEFIELD STREET-1
The main building at the Governor's Inn was built in 1920 by Huntley Spaulding (1869–1955) and is referred to as "the Huntley." It has a high *hip roof* with three dormers, five *bays* and *blind arches* over the first-floor windows. The shallow arch in the entry porch is mirrored in the *fanlight* over the door. I love those swanky awnings. The detail of the elliptical staircase is from the Huntley.

### WAKEFIELD STREET-2
In the early 1920s, Huntley's younger brother, Rolland Spaulding (1873–1942), built this home, known as "the Rolland Estate." The building features a high gable roof, paired end chimneys, seven *bays*, paneled shutters, a side wing and a beautiful arched entry porch. It retains the original slate roof.

Arguably, these two structures are among the finest pairs of Georgian Revival houses in the country. This is especially noteworthy given that they were built and simultaneously occupied by two brothers, both of whom were New Hampshire governors.

Wakefield Street-2

Wakefield Street-3

## WAKEFIELD STREET-3

The Gafney Home resembles a medieval keep, the stronghold at the center of a castle. It is a rare example of Romanesque Revival in residential architecture, with its burly masonry construction and assertive rounded features: a circular corner *tower*, a curving wall, conical roof elements and a semicircular arch at the entry. The sills and *lintels* are made of rough faced granite while the *quoins* are of smooth granite. The Romanesque period ran from roughly the sixth to the twelfth century, commencing some time after the fall of Rome in AD 476 and preceding the Gothic period.

The building incorporates some surprising Colonial Revival elements: that squat *Palladian window* in the dormer and the delicate wooden porch oddly bifurcated by the brick *frontispiece*. Note the floral terra cotta above the entry arch.

The stained-glass window is situated above the landing (not visible from the front). Sumptuous, dark woodwork inside the building is retained in its natural condition; the detailing on the interior of the Governor's Inn, on the other hand, has been painted an elegant off white.

# The Gafney Home for the Aged

The house was built in 1897 by distinguished Rochester attorney and county probate judge Charles Gafney. Gafney, orphaned at the age of four, was wounded at the Battle of Petersburg in the Civil War ("The War of the Rebellion," as it was described in a 1942 booklet about the house, or "The Recent Unpleasantness," as my friends in Beaufort, South Carolina, refer to it).

Judge Gafney and his wife died soon after the house was built. He stipulated in his will that the property be designated for a charitable purpose. The trustees conveyed it to the Gafney Home for the Aged, which opened in 1904. The Gafney Home is an assisted-living, supported residential-care facility, meaning that it provides lifetime care for seniors. According to Ruth Gilbert, the administrator, ten ladies and three gentlemen currently live in the home. She says that they take such good care of the residents that they live a long time. I believe her: the youngest fellow is eighty-eight and there are two centenarians!

An excerpt from the 1942 booklet regarding Rules and Regulations adopted January 1, 1904, states that the inhabitants "must endeavor, by

Wakefield Street-3

gentle and courteous deportment to diffuse an air of cheerfulness and good feeling throughout the Home and by acts of kindness and forbearance, to gain the esteem and promote the comfort and happiness of each other."

From my several visits to the Gafney Home, I can attest that the residents appear to be in full compliance.

# FRISBIE MEMORIAL HOSPITAL

*When I am working on a problem I never think about beauty. I only think
about how to solve the problem. But when I have finished, if the solution is not
beautiful, I know it is wrong.*
—*Buckminster Fuller*

Frisbie Memorial Hospital is Rochester's most stalwart local institution. The hospital came into this world in 1916 when Dr. Walter Roberts and Minnie Eagle started the Eagle Hospital at 95 Charles Street, adjacent to Rochester Child Care Center. It had ten beds and four nurses. Two years later, the hospital moved to 58 South Main Street and doubled in size.

In 1929, Dr. Jesse Frisbie left $23,000 to the hospital, which was subsequently renamed in memory of his late son. That bequest and a $200,000 gift years later from the Spaulding family were used to acquire the present site and build a new hospital there in 1940. The original building still stands but it is now engulfed by later buildings.

## WHITEHALL ROAD

The Sarah Kendall Building was completed in 1951. It was one of the earliest structures on the site and served as a dormitory for nurses. Pay was low and nurses worked long hours; it was common at that time for a hospital to provide them with housing. The building is now mainly administrative offices.

This brick Georgian Revival structure is simple in its symmetrical design with six *bays* surmounted by six dormers, corner *quoins* and a central *pavilion*,

Whitehall Road

but it has a solid, dignified presence. The surprisingly steep gable in the middle, however, almost conveys a medieval feel as a foil to its otherwise regimental mien. That bush in the front is the mother of all rhododendrons.

## The Hospital Business

Frisbie is a not-for-profit, acute-care community hospital. There are approximately 3,750 inpatient admissions per year. It has 112 beds and about 1,000 employees in the main hospital. The institution operates satellite medical office buildings in Rochester, Somersworth, Barrington, Farmington and Wakefield.

Most hospitals in New Hampshire are community hospitals, in contrast to specialized hospitals like a children's hospital or cancer center. Community hospitals provide essentially the same services, and where there are numerous such institutions, as in the Seacoast area, there is strong competition. There are no market restrictions imposed by the state. Patients are mobile, they have high expectations and they exercise their freedom to choose services.

Hospital president Al Felgar says that a well-maintained physical plant is fundamental to remaining competitive. Good design conveys a sense of pride, dedication to quality and a commitment to the broader community. In his sixteen years as president, Mr. Felgar has created an outstanding architectural legacy. Here are a few examples.

## Rochester Hill Road-1

This imposing eighty-eight-thousand-square-foot, four-story expansion of the main building was completed in 2008 at a cost of $34,500,000. It houses the Gustafson Women's and Children's Unit, the Behre Coronary Care Unit and a new endoscopy unit. The addition was designed by the firm of Shepley, Bulfinch, Richardson & Abbott.

This structure, in combination with the earlier addition at the lower left, is an exciting piece of architectural sculpture. It is also a study in contrasts: solid sections versus voids created where the building steps back; three dimensional masses, particularly at the upper left, versus the two dimensional plane of the canopy; straight lines of the *eaves* and *hoods* over the windows versus the

Rochester Hill Road-1

Rochester Hill Road-2

Rochester Hill Road-3

curved edge of the canopy and the bending lines in the block to the left of the entry; blank walls versus expanses of glass; and warm brick versus cold metal siding. Definitely a cool building.

## ROCHESTER HILL ROAD-2

The Frisbie Conference and Education Center, built in 2000, is enthralling, sitting high on a knoll over Rochester Hill Road. I consider it the city's finest contemporary structure.

In keeping with its function, the building evokes a lodge or retreat. It is striking for its ground-hugging shape, curving forms, square *hip roof*, roof *monitor* and gallant carriage porch. It incorporates a rich array of materials: stone, brick, natural woods and copper.

The building was designed by Rochester resident Joe Britton of Lavallee/Brensinger Architects. Mr. Britton has done a good deal of work for the hospital, which must be gratifying, as his father was a surgeon at Frisbie and his brother is currently a surgeon there.

## ROCHESTER HILL ROAD-3

The Skyhaven Medical Building is not on the Frisbie campus, but situated opposite Skyhaven Airport. In recent years, hospitals have tended to expand with outlying medical offices due to tight main sites and the desire to reach out to patients. The building is broken into a series of smaller masses that provide human *scale* and variation. It meets the adjacent meadow nicely with its low-slung profile, poised comfortably between the tall grass and the big sky.

# The Rochester Opera House

*Ah…music. A magic beyond all we do here.*
*—Albus Dumbledore, Hogwarts headmaster*

The Rochester Opera House is our most precious jewel. The Opera House occupies the upper floors of city hall. This sublime space is noteworthy for its suspended horseshoe balcony, opulent stage arch, delicate stenciling and murals, as demonstrated in the three photographs shown here.

As lovely as it is, and as fine as the acoustics are, the Opera House is more renowned for its engineering. George Gilman Adams, a Rochester-area native, designed seven buildings in northern New England that combined a city hall and an opera house. Five of those, including Rochester's, incorporated a movable floor system in the opera house. Tragically, the other four were lost to fire. The two other city hall/opera house structures that did not feature a movable floor, in Waterville, Maine, and Montpelier, Vermont, do survive.

## The Amazing Moving Floor!

The floor functions in both an inclined and a level position. It is raised for theatrical and musical productions and lowered for dances, dinners, public meetings and, at one point, high school basketball games. The fifty-seven-foot-wide and forty-nine-foot-long floor is attached at the far end near the stage and rises three feet at the back edge. It operates with a three-horsepower

Stage. *Photograph by Allegra English.*

motor, leather belts, gears, flywheels, one continuous shaft, seven pairs of connecting rods and single-piece floor timbers that run the entire length.

This arrangement, of course, requires two different sets of doors on the back wall. One door at each corner floats preternaturally above the floor when it is in the level position. Then, when the floor is raised, you notice that the other pair of doors in the middle of the back wall are partially sunk. I imagine Harry and Hermione, standing in those doors, waving goodbye as the doors continue their descent below the floor.

No other historic theatre in the country has an inclining floor system like Rochester's. Landis Magnuson, a theatre specialist at St. Anselm College, says that Neche Hall in Neche, North Dakota, was balanced in the middle and could be raised and lowered on both ends like a teeter-totter. He says, however, that those mechanics compared poorly to Rochester's system. St. George Social Hall in St. George, Utah, had a floor that was elevated with four large wooden screws that were turned manually. Unfortunately, that floor is stuck in position today.[*]

---

[*] Landis K. Magnuson, "New England Yankee Ingenuity," *Theater Design & Technology* (Winter 1992), 16–17.

# History of the Opera House

City hall and the 850-seat Opera House (there were more seats originally) were built in 1908, at a cost of $85,745.62. The opening performance on September 4 of that year was the play *Miss Petticoats*. It tells of the tribulations of a young lady who is not aware, until the end of the story, that she is of noble birth. The facility fast became the cultural heart of the community, hosting plays, minstrels, vaudeville shows, singing cowboys, movies, balls and political events.

Spaulding High School, which has a sterling auditorium itself, opened in 1939. With the availability of that space and the increasing popularity of moving pictures, the role of the Opera House diminished. A year later, the Opera House was nearly eviscerated when the Rochester Building Committee proposed removing the floor system and balcony to create two floors of office space. Providentially, the plans were not implemented due to insufficient funds.

The shows went on for another thirty-four years until the final performance of *The Frisbie Follies* in October 1974. Then the doors closed and the Opera House fell into a long slumber.

Orchestra and balcony. *Courtesy of the Rochester Opera House.*

In 1987, the city government sought to reopen the facility. The floor system was broken and its operation was now a mystery. Charles Goodspeed, an engineering professor from the University of New Hampshire, spent several days crawling around under the floor trying to figure out how it worked. The price to repair the system was estimated at $1.2 million. The effort was scrapped.

## Rejuvenation of the Opera House

In 1996, newly elected mayor Harvey Bernier called upon the citizens of Rochester to meet the challenge of restoring the Opera House. Along with the broken floor, the walls and ceiling had been damaged from a leaking roof and layers of paint covered the stenciling. The community responded.

George Allen, a retired engineer and founder of OASIS, a company that provides precision alignment services for printing presses, was appointed chair of a new Opera House committee. According to Mr. Bernier, over $1

Stenciling detail

million worth of materials, professional services and labor was donated. The floor was repaired and the space rejuvenated.

We owe much of the current success of the Opera House to two remarkable volunteers: Susan Page, the multitalented managing director and publicist, and the unsinkable Cathy Taylor, president of the Opera House. Susan has dark hair and does her creative work behind the scenes; Cathy is blonde and possessed of enormous energy and an uproarious laugh. What do they share? They are fiercely devoted to the Opera House and they both love their shoes (this is Rochester, after all).

The Rochester Opera House is now a thriving regional entertainment venue. It showcases acts like Natalie McMaster, Dave Brubeck, Beatlemania, the Shanghai Circus and Charo, the cuchi-cuchi girl who happens to be a world-class flamenco guitarist, as well as local performances like Seacoast Dancing with the Stars and the Nutcracker Suite. We are pleased to note that the Opera House is, once more, most assuredly, the cultural heart of this community.

# Part 3

# OTHER ARCHITECTURAL ELEMENTS

# The Front Porch

*The best kind of friend is the kind you can sit on a porch swing with,*
*never say a word [to], then walk away feeling like*
*it was the best conversation that you ever had.*
—*anonymous*

Consider the many classic movies with crucial scenes set on a front porch: *To Kill a Mockingbird*, *The Long Hot Summer*, *The Great Santini* and *The Big Chill*, to name a few. The fellow finally kisses his gal, Dad tells an instructive parable, long-suppressed anger emerges or two buddies just rock without speaking. Porches were more common in the South, to be sure, but they also played a role in the lives of us Yankees. Clint Eastwood spent hours on the porch in *Gran Torino*, though, admittedly, it did not induce much conviviality on his part.

## Outdoor Room

The streets in front of our homes and businesses are our most pervasive shared space. In older neighborhoods, streets serve multiple functions. They are a place for children to play; a place to hang out and socialize; and a place to walk, ride bicycles or drive cars (maybe not exactly in that order). The renowned architect Louis Kahn said, "In a city the street must be supreme. It is the first institution of the city. The street is a room by agreement, a community room, the walls [formed by buildings] of which belong to the donors, dedicated to the city for common use. Its ceiling is the sky."

A satisfying sense of enclosure is created. Street trees reinforce this effect, their trunks being the walls and their canopies, the ceilings. I believe that human beings crave space that enfolds them in this manner; it elicits feelings of safety and peacefulness.

The *focal point* of this outdoor room is the front porch, which, like the gallery above a theatre stage, animates the street. You can be outside and enjoy the parade of activity, and at the same time savor the solitude of your home. Porches have this pleasing ambiguity. Be a spectator or a participant. Invite a chap to join you for lemonade. Then, when you tire of his company, send him off without offense by simply retiring into your house.

The porch must be properly configured. It needs to be close to the sidewalk so that you can actually have a conversation with people walking by, but it should not be too close, and it should be raised up so that you have a secure feeling of separation. A porch must be wide and at least six or eight feet deep, so that you can stretch out a little. Please don't screen it or enclose it. Create that Florida or California room somewhere else.

Front porches are rarely built on houses today. There is not much worth watching in the street other than cars racing by. Plus, the house is set so far back and the street is so wide that you couldn't converse with passersby, anyway. Rather than stipulating a minimum front setback in our zoning ordinances, we should mandate a maximum setback, also called a "build-to line." Another benefit of narrow streets is that they calm traffic, planner-speak for slowing it down.

Andres Duany says, "America's public spaces are sized by the biggest fire engine the community can afford to buy." The problem is exacerbated when the chiefs go to annual conventions and compare the sizes of their ladder trucks. The guy with the smaller truck comes home and feels compelled to buy a bigger one. Then the town has to ream out the streets to make room for it. We need to hire more female fire chiefs.

Today, many people seek privacy over a sense of belonging. Prior to the advent of air conditioning, especially in southern coastal towns, you went to your porch to enjoy the cooling summer breezes. Now that there is no privy in the backyard, homeowners can build decks and patios there instead of retiring to the front of the house.

# Other Architectural Elements

Charles Street

Broad Street

Eastern Avenue

## Charles Street

This house has a full-width porch with widely spaced columns. Note that a proper front porch, like the *classical* porch, has an even number of columns (except on wraparound porches). It is the spaces framed by the columns, rather than the columns themselves, that contain our attention. Therefore, the center of the porch, which is the *focal point*, should be occupied by this space and not by a single column, which cannot absorb us in the same way. In addition, having an odd number of spaces establishes a hierarchy, with the space in the middle being dominant, which is more satisfying than a duality, i.e., two equal halves without a strong center.

Picket fences, like the one shown here, are another useful device that the new urbanists have revived. The picket fence neatly demarcates the public realm of the street and sidewalk and the private realm of one's yard and home. Yet it does so gently—with a permeable "wall" like that formed by the columns of a porch—so that the homeowner and the person strolling by, again, can communicate in a safely defined but casual way.

# Other Architectural Elements

## BROAD STREET

This curved wraparound porch is classic Victorian with its turned posts, decorative *brackets* and *balustrade*. I love that disheveled dude in front, holding court from his rocking chair.

## EASTERN AVENUE

The Studley Home has a grand wraparound porch with double columns and a *pediment* at the entry. Now there's a fine spot to while away the afternoon.

# SIGNS

*You can tell the ideals of a nation by its advertisements.*
*—Norman Douglas, British writer*

We try to ignore the clutter and cacophony of signs along the road. Most are forgettable, if not offensive, but some are truly distinguished and rightfully capture our attention.

Different signage is appropriate for different settings. Larger, brighter, bolder designs are acceptable on commercial corridors that are geared to motorists, like Route 11 and Route 125. There are even a handful of places, such as Times Square and downtown Tokyo, where we applaud the outlandish display. Urban, sensitive, pedestrian-oriented and scenic locations, however, call for restrained signage.

It would be a fine thing for us to demand higher quality in the small details that compose our public realm, including signs. Paul Spreiregen says, "Urban design is…the exercise of artistry in every detail of city building… [t]he bridges and roads that bring us to the city, the benches we sit on, the places where we wait for buses, the places where children play, the places where we browse for books, where we have our shoes shined, the lights that illuminate our cities, and the signs that give us directions."[*]

Restaurants, banks, specialty stores, medical offices, law firms, churches, public and nonprofit institutions and businesses such as florists and printing companies generally nurture a more refined image and tend to purchase high-quality signage.

---

[*] Spreiregen, *Urban Design*, 104.

*Above, left*: Farmington Road

*Above, right*: Wakefield Street

# Illumination

Lighting is an important factor in a sign's character. Signs may be <u>externally illuminated</u>—lit by a stationary bulb projecting onto the sign; <u>internally illuminated</u>—where a translucent plastic sign is lit from the inside; or made with <u>neon</u>—exposed tubes filled with a gas that glows when electrified. Often streetlights or other area lights provide sufficient lighting such that the sign need not be lit at all.

Many internally illuminated signs are objectionable due to their use of plastic, excessive size, tawdry design and too frequent use of white, yellow or other bright colors that cause glare at night. It is unfortunate that many enterprises seek to gain not our admiration, but rather our attention, by metaphorically screaming at us.

Do not confuse neon with internal illumination. Neon is low-key, retro and cool. Think smoky jazz or a diner in an Edward Hopper painting. Neon gas is actually orange-red. Different gases are used to produce the other colors, though we refer to it all as "neon." This type of signage is, unfortunately, not used much anymore.

Tragically, we are now being assaulted by a horrendous new generation of advertising: electronic message signs. These are like JumboTrons, the large screens used in sports stadiums, with their frantic flashing, pounding, pumping, popping, pulsating images. They are a scourge and should be prohibited. At a minimum, severe restrictions should be placed on their operation. It is legal to do so, at least in New Hampshire, where the state supreme court upheld a ban by the City of Concord.

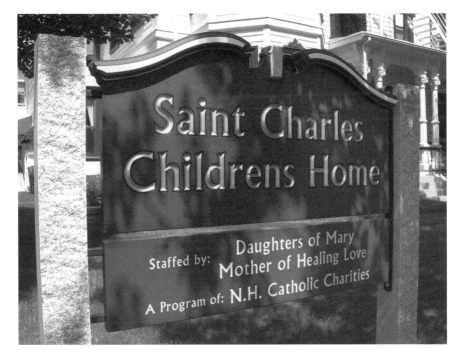

Grant Street

## Handcrafted Signage

Nearly all signs are tailor made. A good sign embodies one or more of the following features: it is simple and tasteful; it is expressive, evocative or playful; it has deep, dark, rich colors; it uses an attractive typeface; it uses good materials.

The Jenny Wren and Saint Charles Children's Home signs use real gold leaf. Ernie "Redwood" Shipman, proprietor of Renaissance Signs in Gonic, explained how it is applied. Gold, usually twenty-three-carat gold (twenty-four-carat is 100 percent pure gold), is purchased in packets of tissue-thin three- by three-inch squares. A varnish is placed on the bare wood and left to dry overnight to acquire a sticky quality. The gold is then brushed onto the varnish; it is too delicate to be touched with one's hand. No coating is placed over it because gold does not tarnish or wear away. A thief would not be tempted to try to steal it off a sign, as the amount that could be collected would be virtually worthless.

Mr. Shipman said there is no paint, not even any metallic paint, that can achieve this luster. When asked why that was, Ernie just smiled and said,

North Main Street

"It's gold." One also sees what appears to be silver leaf on signs occasionally. Actually, platinum, a metallic element, is used to create this effect, as real silver would tarnish.

Traditionally, the highest quality outdoor signs are made of wood, mainly redwood and mahogany. These two woods are dimensionally stable and resistant to rot and decay. They hold paint and varnish well. And, of course, they are beautiful. Most mahogany is now imported from plantations in Latin America. Unfortunately, redwood is too slow growing to be raised in a nursery, so much of it comes from old growth trees.

The price of redwood and mahogany has risen, and therefore urethane, a synthetic material, is used increasingly. It is durable and easy to work and, when painted, it resembles wood. Nonetheless, I don't expect Ernie Shipman's nickname to change any time soon.

# CEMETERIES

*There's no reason to be the richest man in the cemetery.*
*You can't do any business there.*
*—Colonel Harlan Sanders, fried chicken tycoon*

I know of no other setting that is at once so beautiful and stimulating, yet so meditative. Cemeteries showcase sculpture, calligraphy, poetry and horticulture; they are bird sanctuaries and arboretums; and they teach us social history.

It is moving to contemplate the difficult lives of our forebears as told by their tombstones. A couple loses several small children, likely to illness. A man survives three young wives, each presumably having died in childbirth. A woman outlives her husband, perhaps killed in war, by over forty years.

## Rochester's Cemeteries

One local resident is working to preserve these underappreciated resources. In 1990, Richard Longo was asked by the late mayor Roland Roberge to inventory all of the cemeteries in the city. So far, he has identified 128, including these municipal burial grounds: three sections of the Rochester Cemetery on Franklin Street, including the mournful original section that is hidden behind U-Haul; Haven Hill Cemetery on Route 108; Poor Farm Cemetery, set up for the indigent, in front of Home Depot; Gonic Cemetery; and Old Cold Springs Cemetery in East Rochester.

There are 117 family graveyards and four church cemeteries: St. Mary's, Holy Rosary, St. Leo's and the Friends. The Legro family burial ground, situated inside the cloverleaf at Exit 15, is being relocated as part of the Spaulding Turnpike widening project. When asked which burial grounds are the most interesting, Mr. Longo replied, "Every cemetery has a story."

The vast majority of family graveyards are abandoned, and many are now maintained by the city government. Waste Management Company, under the leadership of former president Bob Steele, restored eight family cemeteries located on its property. Relatives may still be buried in family graveyards, including abandoned ones, but otherwise, interments today are permitted only in established public or church cemeteries.

Stephen Roy is one of the few remaining stone engravers in the area. Mr. Roy learned the trade from his grandfather and still does some handwork. The standard process now, though, uses high technology. He designs on a computer, selecting a typeface and an image from among thousands available. The computer directs a plotter that cuts out a stencil design on a rubber blanket. The blanket is attached to the stone and sandblasted. The high-pressure sand bounces off the blanket but cuts into the exposed granite. His is a demanding business, calling for artistry, physical toughness and sensitivity in dealing with the bereaved.

# Funerary Art

Many of the earliest gravestones in New England were made of slate. It split readily into slabs and was relatively easy to cut. Fortuitously, these stones have been long-lasting. Marble and soapstone, commonly used in the nineteenth century, are, unfortunately, subject to serious erosion. Most monuments today are made of granite, a very hard material.

Funerary art reveals changing attitudes toward death. Early tombstones in New England typically contained forbidding images of the finality of death, such as a skeleton, a skull and crossbones, a winged skull, a body in a casket, an hourglass or a clock. "Memento mori," Latin for "Remember death," was a common inscription.

## SALLY MARCH

Later stones in the colonial period expressed the longing for a gentle afterlife, with a winged cherub or an odd juxtaposition of the deceased's face attached to a pair of wings. Hope for the continuity of life was depicted in fertility symbols, vines and sunbursts. About 1800, a melancholy perspective emerged with the widespread image of a weeping willow tree and an urn, which symbolizes nature grieving. This grim and grammatically challenged epitaph from 1811 reads, "Fair passenger who passest by, Look on this stone & learn to die, In midst of life, with sudden stroke, Life's fairest hopes are often broke."

## Eda May Meader

Surprisingly, the Eda May Meader marker, which resembles slate, is metal. This monument was probably purchased by mail order. The frame would have been mass produced, with a metal insert specially crafted for the individual. The tender epitaph reads, "Sleep, dear loved one sleep, Lif's [*sic*] rocky steeps are past, and in pastures green, by waters still, thy tired feet rest at last."

## Tree Tunnel

Cemeteries reached full flower in the Victorian age. Mount Auburn Cemetery in Cambridge, Massachusetts, was founded in 1831 as the first garden cemetery. With its superlative monuments, ornamental plantings and fountains, Mount Auburn was intended to be a place for the living as well as the dead. It was the inspiration for the design of innumerable other cemeteries, including, most likely, Rochester Cemetery's tree tunnel.

## Richardson

Imposing monuments were erected by those who could afford them. Columns, often broken or draped, were commonly used. Because of their elaborate death rituals, the forms developed by the ancient Egyptians, including the *obelisk*, which was carved with hieroglyphics, became standard funerary symbols. Some *monolithic* obelisks, over one hundred feet tall and made of a single piece of granite, were floated on the Nile River to their destinations. The obelisk of the Richardson memorial is a powerful *focal point*.

## Houle

Leaves and flowers are used for symbolic purposes. The rose, of course, signifies love and also eternal joy but, at the same time, grief. The *acanthus* leaf, which adorns *Corinthian capitals*, represents heavenly gardens. Oak leaves symbolize strength or endurance, and laurel leaves represent victory. Ivy is associated with death and eternal life. It also symbolizes memory and fidelity.

Sally March

Eda May Meader

Tree tunnel

Richardson

Houle

The stem on the Houle stone appears to be a bald cypress, not a traditional sign, but an apt one. The bald cypress is the only conifer, other than the larch tree, that drops all of its needles.

## SCRUTON

A computer-guided laser etched a beautiful farm scene onto the Scruton stone. Tombstones are now sometimes hand painted as well. Photographic images of the deceased may also be rendered in porcelain and permanently affixed to the stone.

## FRENCH HUSSEY

Staples, the office supply company, recently built a new store on Washington Street. All of the headstones from the French Hussey family cemetery, located on the site, had been removed by a prior property owner. The Flatley Company, developer of the project, restored the cemetery, installing landscaping and a granite and metal rail fence. Mr. Longo secured an abandoned stone, on which Stephen Roy engraved "French Hussey" and the names of those buried there (on the back of the stone).

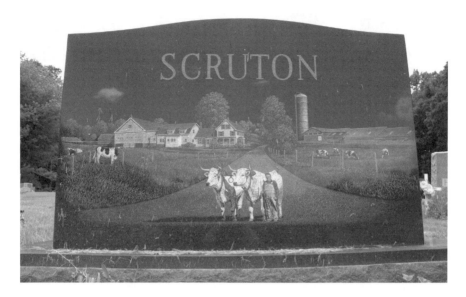

Scruton

French Hussey

# Other Architectural Elements

A gravestone is crafted to memorialize a unique individual, sometimes with a token of whatever gave that person joy in his or her life: a sailboat, a flock of birds, a devotional symbol, a Red Sox cap. The function of cemeteries is to provide a tranquil setting for the deceased and a place for their loved ones to feel some connection. They quietly, but graciously, beckon the rest of us to visit also, however briefly.

# STONE WALLS

Ideally, agricultural soil is deep, rich and loamy, but that was not the ground on which New England farmers toiled. They joked that they could grow stones more easily than any other crop, since plowing a field pushes to the surface new stones that had been buried before.

Stone walls were a phenomenon mainly of the Northeast and Middle Atlantic states, but many were built farther west by Yankee farmers who resettled there. Most were built from 1775 to 1840. It is estimated that there were once 240,000 miles of stone walls in New England. This length exceeds the distance to the moon, at perigee, the shortest distance. The Great Wall of China continues for a mere 4,000 miles.

Stones are individual, loose fragments broken off from rock, which is the unified mass of bedrock that composes the earth's crust (thus the proper term is indeed "stone wall" rather than "rock wall"). As the glaciers grew and advanced toward the south, they abraded and removed bedrock. Then, as they melted and retreated north, they deposited stones and boulders, mixed with soil. This is why you might occasionally see one huge stone, aptly called an "erratic," in the middle of a forest with no other sizable stones nearby.

Farmers had to remove the stones in order to work their land, but at least the stones were put to good use. The walls they built fenced in their animals,

Rochester Hill Road

prevented stray animals from eating their crops, demarcated different parts of their fields and marked their property boundaries. Livestock pens were often created inside the parcel of land, so stone walls did not necessarily identify property boundaries.

# A Brief History of Agriculture in New England

The earliest settlements in New England were in low-lying coastal and river areas that had sandy soils. As people moved inland, the soils were stonier, so more walls were built. After the Revolution, there was a significant increase in population, and agriculture expanded accordingly.

In 1810, William Jarvis, the American consul to Portugal, brought over four thousand merino sheep to his Vermont farm. Merino sheep, bred by the Portuguese, were prized for their soft, high-quality wool. Sheep farming became the rage in New England for the next thirty years. During this time, an unprecedented amount of forest was converted to sheep pasture, accompanied by a great wave of stone wall construction.

The year 1840 was a high-water mark. In that year, there were 600,000 sheep in New Hampshire, more than two for each of the state's 285,000 residents. Long-held beliefs in some quarters that farmers in the early nineteenth century engaged in livestock cloning have been validated by recent research confirming that fully one third of those sheep were named Dolly.

New England farms were overgrazed by 1840, causing serious erosion and ultimately exposing much of the bedrock that we see today. Large-scale sheep farming ended shortly afterward. There was then a mass migration toward the Ohio River Valley and other places in the west. Significant transportation improvements in canals, railroads and turnpikes drew people off the farms toward the growing cities. By the Great Depression, the majority of family farms in the region had been abandoned.

Most of the New England landscape had been cleared by 1840, leaving less than 25 percent forested. This was likely the point at which the region had its lowest level of forest cover in human history. From that time forward, agricultural land continually gave way to tree cover, and today, about 83 percent of the state is forested. It is now slowly being deforested again, but for development rather than farming.

Wire fencing was introduced about 1840, supplanting stone walls as the preferred method for identifying land. Barbed wire was invented in the 1870s. If you would like to know more about this particular subject, run, don't walk, to the Kansas Museum of Barbed Wire in LaCrosse, Kansas.

# Moving the Stones

Generally, as the farmer worked his field, he placed the unearthed stones on a wooden sled called a stoneboat, which his horses then pulled to the location where the wall would be erected. Robert Thorson, author of several books on stone walls, says, "For New England farmers, the sphere is the worst possible shape for a stone; it is easy to overlook in the subsoil (waiting to break a plow tip), hard to grub out (its center of mass is deep), difficult to transport on a vehicle (it is likely to roll off), and hard to carry (its center of mass must be held far away from the center of the body). It is also the worst shape...[for] wall construction because spheres don't stack well…The only advantage of spheres is that big ones can be more easily rolled to the edge of a field."*

When there were more stones than could be used, the farmer might pile them into a cairn in a corner of his field. Sometimes, mice made homes in these piles. The cairn terrier was specially bred to flush them out.

# Building the Wall

Robert Thorson says, "Every wall that's more than a dump of stone is a piece of folk art, reflecting the idiosyncratic, artistic impulse of its builder."†
The quality of the wall is largely the result of how tightly the stones fit together and the extent to which distinct horizontal lines are created.

In building a wall, sometimes a trench would be dug and filled with gravel to prevent the wall from shifting. Large stones were, naturally, positioned on the bottom. Flat stones, called "capstones," were placed on top. Nearly all stone walls are thigh high because humans are weaker working above this level.

Most walls are one stone wide. A double wall has two walls composed of regular, workable stones with misshapen rubble placed in the middle space. *Thrufters* were wide, flat stones used to bridge the gap periodically between the two outer walls. Make up creative, new ways to use this funny word and see if it catches on, as in, "I drive an old thrufter," or, "There is a nest of triple-tufted thrufters in my backyard."

Virtually all stone walls built along farm fields are *dry walls*, built without mortar. There would be no reason to add it to dumped walls, and its use would undercut the artistry of building a laid wall. A little mortar was occasionally placed on top to better hold the wall together, reduce infiltration of water or prevent theft.

John Nolan, editor of the *Rochester Times*, wrote an article a few years ago about Philip Zaeder, a retired English teacher in Milton, New Hampshire, who enjoys mending old stone walls: "'I have learned to respect the gravity of granite and the contours of the land'…While mending walls, Zaeder says he finds a new way of being mindful, without being full of ideas and reasons. He is aware of the soil's smell and the scent of leaves. 'You can only work with deliberation, stone by stone. It is the world being put to right,' he said."‡

Philip Zaeder is a stone wall whisperer.

---

* Thorson, *Exploring Stone Walls*, 25.
† Ibid., 66.
‡ John Nolan, "Zaeder Treads in the Footsteps of Frost," *Rochester Times*, February 11, 2007.

Four Rod Road

## Rochester Hill Road

This view over the Gagne Farm has been preserved through a conservation easement donated by Gaye Nadeau and Richard Gagne. Their family retains ownership of the land and can still farm or log it. However, the development rights were conveyed to a nonprofit organization, thereby permanently protecting the land. The cells marked by stone walls were used to grow different crops.

## Four Rod Road

Wade Scribner recently built this beautiful double stone wall in front of his house.

Stone walls are part of the built environment, but once abandoned, they fall to nature's caprice. Animals make homes in them, trees grow around them, gravity pulls them down and moss and lichen swathe them. When I wander into a New England wood, it is stirring to encounter an old stone wall. Incongruously situated in the forest, rather than in the open field that it originally bounded, the wall seems a mysterious remnant from some civilization long since vanished.

# THE STONE ARCH BRIDGE

*An arch never sleeps.*
*—James Fergusson, architectural author*

We move now from *dry wall* to *wet wall* construction, using mortar. The Stone Arch Bridge, spanning the Cocheco River right in our downtown, is in rarefied company. It was built in 1883, the same year as the more high-flying Brooklyn Bridge.

It is surprising to learn that behind the granite, the underlying bridge is composed of brick *vaults*. Earthen material fills the space over the vaulting. Gravel sits on the earthen fill and is covered, in turn, with the road pavement. Silas Hussey, a local quarryman and stonecutter, built the bridge; he hired mason Henry Wilkinson to construct the brick vaults.

## Arches

The structure of the bridge is fairly simple. It is supported by three equally sized, shaped and spaced arches, *vaults* actually, that transfer weight to the vertical piers and *abutments*. It would be out of character if I didn't go off on some foray at this late stage, so forthwith, a brief tour of arches.

Arches and vaults are composed of wedge-shaped blocks called *voussoirs*. They are not self supporting until the last voussoir, called the *keystone*, is placed at the top. Voussoirs are laid and mortared along arched wood scaffolding, called *centering*, which supports the arch until it can stand on its own.

Moving from highest to lowest arches, the tall *pointed arch* is used in Gothic architecture. The most recognizable is the semicircular or half-round (or simply round) arch. Visualize a Roman aqueduct. Most of the arches in the "Government Buildings" chapter are round arches.

The most elegant is the *elliptical arch*. A chicken's egg, in two dimensions, is an ellipse, though not a perfect one, since one end is slightly pointed. Slice the egg in half (carefully!) longitudinally and the top half forms an elliptical arch. It is the only standard arch that is not composed of one or more segments of a circle. Rather, the elliptical curve is a wonderful mathematical construct where the radius continually changes. For that reason, it is difficult to build well. The Jenny Wren and Café signs are ellipses.

The *basket arch* is a poor man's elliptical arch, and you have to look carefully to distinguish the two. This arch is composed of three curves: a larger, flatter one on top and smaller, tighter ones on each side. The Stone Arch Bridge is composed of *segmental arches*, which are segments of less than half of a circle. This is one of the easiest types of arches to build, and one of the most stable. It is not as pleasing as the basket arch because the latter approaches vertical at its two ends, where it meets the adjoining wall or pier. There are segmental *pediments* on three buildings in the "Contemporary Commercial Styles" section.

Then there is the *flat arch*, an oxymoron like "peacekeeper missile" or "tight slacks." It is not really an arch though it functions like one. Its *voussoirs* are placed horizontally across the opening like a *lintel*, but their outward splay transfers the downward forces above, horizontally away from the center. There are flat arches over the windows of the Sarah Kendall Building in the "Frisbie Memorial Hospital" chapter.

# Bridge Aesthetics

Structural engineering was not an exact science in the nineteenth century, so masonry structures like the Stone Arch Bridge were significantly overbuilt. This is one reason they usually have an especially long life span. The large, rough-face blocks give the Stone Arch Bridge a commanding presence, yet its elongated profile and shallow arches lend it some polish. Old photographs and postcards depict a more delicate railing providing a striking contrast to the heavy masonry.

The appearance of the bridge varies as the water level rises and falls. Shadows also change depending on the time of day and one's vantage point. Note that, as in the case of porches and columns (see section "The Front Porch"), an odd number of arches is more satisfying than an even number.

Bridges should need no embellishment to be beautiful, as their naked physics are beautiful. Here is where modernist principles are most poignant. Yet there is opportunity for banality with contemporary bridges because the strength and *monolithic* nature of concrete and steel does not require elegance in design.

Frederick Gottemoeller, an expert on bridge design, said,

> *Unfortunately, most everyday bridges convey a message of apathy and mediocrity. Carrying traffic but lacking grace, they are merely functional. They could be much more. They could be works of civic art which would enliven each day's travels and make everyone's journey more pleasant. Bridges have the ability to arouse emotions like wonder, awe, surprise, or sheer enjoyment of form and color.*[*]

I am pleased to note that the City of Rochester is currently planning the complete rehabilitation of this memorable structure.

---

[*] Gottemoeller, *Bridgescape*, preface, 4.

# THE DOORS OF ROCHESTER

*To invite a person into your house is to take charge of his happiness for as long as he is under your roof.*
*—Anthelme Brillat-Savarin, French epicure*

You may have seen that poster "The Doors of Dublin," which depicts beautiful entryways in Dublin, Ireland. I propose a similar poster for Rochester. Imagine these doors in all of their resplendent colors.

For the entrance, every color is welcome, as long as it has personality. Red is rightly popular for its sensuality. Black is handsome, formal and a little edgy. Orange is luminous and gregarious. Yellow promotes good cheer and *gemütlichkeit*. White, especially where matching a fine portico, is pristine. Blue is serene. Green expresses balance and harmony. Brown, whether in natural wood or painted, evokes the richness of the earth. Purple, or better yet, lilac, is the mystical color.

# CONCLUSION

*Be well, do good work, and keep in touch.*
*—Garrison Keillor*

The topics covered here under the rubric of the built environment have been comprehensive. I did consider other elements: tree houses, weather vanes, picket fences, street furniture, statues, abandoned municipal roads. My coworker, Ea Ksander, jokingly suggested that I reprise my original series with an April Fool's Day piece showcasing the best of Rochester's electronic message signs, currently a controversial subject in town.

Indeed, in the course of that series, six years ago, *Rochester Times* editor John Nolan had to rein in some of my cockamamie ideas: "John, how about a piece on Rochester's finest catch basins?" He would remind me that the series was not about Rochester's blemishes, of which, I admit, we have a few, but rather about its jewels, which are countless.

I never did say specifically why I love architecture. Of course, I was enamored by more of Europe than just the Gothic cathedrals. In appreciating the built environment, I am constantly stimulated. Look around. It envelops us like the shingles of a Queen Anne house or the moss on an ancient stone wall. We are housed in a vast outdoor museum showcasing the history of western civilization. Exploring Rochester, just an old shoe town, I am only a few degrees of separation from the pharaohs of Egypt, Louis XIV, Christopher Wren or Andrea Palladio (as if I could escape him, given his ubiquitous windows).

## Conclusion

Contemplate the wondrous legacy of your own community. Then, write a letter to the newspaper to protest some shoddy new building. Tell the board of selectmen to build more sidewalks. Join your local historic district commission or planning board. Now that you are versed in the built environment, become a voice for good design.

On the other hand, that may not be your style. If this book serves simply to enhance your daily life a little as you walk around town, perhaps bringing a knowing smile when you recognize the arches and quoins on a public edifice, then I will be delighted to think that I contributed to that experience.

# ACKNOWLEDGEMENTS

*I feel a very unusual sensation—if it is not indigestion,*
*I think it must be gratitude.*
*—Benjamin Disraeli*

I would like to extend a most warm thank-you to the following people:

The wonderful ladies at 27 Edgewood: Naomi, Liza, Emily and Luna.

Gail Behrendt, whose "hair like a well-fed fire" was catnip to the pazzi ragazzi in Rome.

Irwin Behrendt, who would have been delighted by this book.

The dazzling Doug Decker, who generously shared his knowledge about writing with me. He is a jewel of Nute High School.

Our comrades—(Deb Lerme Goodman and John Goodman)—for teaching me about commas and making me kill way too many of my darlings.

John Nolan, dauntless editor of the *Rochester Times*, for his sagacious guidance throughout the original series.

Art Guadano, Nick Isaac, Brian Ladd, Chip Noon, Monte Pearson and Andrea Simpson who kindly reviewed my manuscript.

# ACKNOWLEDGEMENTS

Maryanna E. Hatch for graciously granting me permission to use the marvelous mural by her late husband, John Hatch, on the cover.

Allegra English for sharing her gorgeous photograph of the Opera House.

Our lovely friend, Eve Edelstein, for trusting me with her Nikon.

Kenn Ortmann, my world-class boss. He is Yoda with a bow tie.

The terrific women in the Planning Department: Madeleine Carter, Cecile Cormier, Ea Ksander (who will note I used the word "myriad" only once) and Caroline Lewis. It hurt to lose the hippo's muumuu.

Terry Desjardins and the Planning Board, dedicated stewards of our built environment.

Nel Sylvain and the Historic District Commission, who deftly and diplomatically promote excellence in design.

Cathy Taylor and Susan Page for ensuring that our magnificent Opera House continues to thrive.

Art Nickless, da man of Norway Plains Associates; Joseph Shields, vice-president of Frisbie Hospital; and Michael Hopkins, Rochester School superintendent.

Paul Marks, my lecturer at the BAC, wherever you might be, and Polly Flansburgh, founder of Boston by Foot.

The New Urbanists, who are slowly changing the world.

My fellow city planners, who always fight the good fight.

Chuck Bulfinch, Hank Richardson, Dick Hunt, Stan White, FLW, Ictinus and Callicrates.

Brianna Cullen and Hilary McCullough, my patient and thoughtful editors, and the other fabulous people at The History Press.

And my mom. Thanks again for turning me on to Westminster Abbey.

# GLOSSARY

**abutment**: The supporting wall at the outer end of a bridge.

**acanthus** (□-căn'-th□s): A plant native to the Mediterranean area whose leaves adorn Corinthian columns.

**arcaded**: Marked by a series of small arches.

**architrave** (är'-k□-tr□v): The lowest part of a classical entablature, resting directly on the columns.

**atlantes**: Columns sculpted in the form of male figures.

**baluster** (băl'-□s-tûr): An upright, often vase-shaped, support for a handrail.

**balustrade** (băl'-□s-tr□d): A handrail supported by a row of balusters.

**basket arch**: An arch composed of three curves, a larger one on top and smaller ones on each side.

**bastard hip**: A hip roof with two different pitches.

**battered**: A structure, such as a column, which tapers as it rises.

**bay**: A vertical rank of windows and doors on a façade.

**bay window**: A bay that has one or more windows and projects outward from the building face.

**belfry**: A structure, usually on a church, containing the bell.

**belt course**: A decorative, horizontal band around a building, usually defining an interior floor level.

**blind arch**: An arch, articulated within a wall, that does not contain an opening for a window or door.

**bow/bowfront**: A curved section projecting outward from a façade.

**bracket**: A supporting element under the eaves, often more decorative than structural.

**broken**: An arch, pediment or other element that is not continuous.

**capital**: The decorated crown of a column or pilaster.

**cartouche** (cär-t□sh'): An ornamental panel in the form of a scroll, circle or oval, often bearing an inscription.

**caryatid** (kâr-□-ăt'-□d): A column sculpted in the form of a female figure.

**casement window**: A window with the sash hung on vertical hinges that opens outward.

**centering**: Temporary scaffolding for an arch or vault, on which the masonry is supported until the keystone is placed and the mortar sets.

**cheek block**: A horizontal block next to a set of entry steps.

**chink**: Material inserted to fill small gaps.

**classical**: The period or style of ancient Greece and Rome.

**clerestory window**: An upper-story window that illuminates an interior multistory space from above.

**colonette**: A thin column.

**compound arch**: A recess of nested arches.

**corbel**: A bracket or block projecting from the face of a wall supporting a cornice.

**Corinthian**: The most ornate of the classical Greek orders, characterized by capitals with stylized acanthus leaves.

**cornerboard**: Vertical board at the corner of a building.

**cornice**: The topmost section of an entablature or the projecting molding at the top of a wall.

**cross gable**: A gable oriented perpendicular to the main roof.

**cupola**: Ornamental structure surmounting a roof, often with a dome.

**curtain wall**: A nonstructural outer skin.

**dentil**: A tooth-like block under the eaves.

**Doric**: The oldest and simplest of the classical Greek orders.

**dry wall**: A masonry wall built without mortar.

**eave**: The projecting overhang at the lower edge of a roof.

**ecclesiastical**: Pertaining to a church.

**elevation**: A drawing of the front façade, sides or rear of a building.

**elliptical arch**: An arch shaped like half of an ellipse, cut longitudinally.

**entablature**: In classical architecture, the part of a structure between the columns and the roof, composed of an architrave, frieze and cornice.

**entasis** (ĕn'-t□-s□s): The slight outward swell in a column.

**eyebrow**: A motif with a shallow arch.

**fanlight**: A fan-shaped window, often set over a door.

**fenestration**: The arrangement of windows on a façade.

**festoon**: An ornamental hanging composed of fruit, flowers or leaves, suspended between two points. *See swag.*

**finial** (f□n'-□-□l): A vertical ornament fixed to the peak of a building.

**flat arch**: A lintel composed of individual voussoirs.

**fluting**: Vertical grooves around the shaft of a column.

**focal point**: A prominent object or element intended to draw one's attention, such as a porch, embellished entrance, fountain, obelisk or statue.

**frieze**: The middle section of an entablature, often decorated with carvings.

**frontispiece**: An ornamental projecting section of a façade.

**gambrel roof**: A roof with two slopes on each side, the lower slope having the steeper pitch.

**golden section**: The ratio of approximately five to eight.

**header**: The narrow side of a brick.

**high style**: Elaborate version of a particular style. *See vernacular.*

**hip roof**: A roof with four uniformly pitched sides.

**hood**: Decorative element over a window.

**hyphen**: A small section of a building linking two larger sections.

**Ionic**: An order of Greek architecture characterized by a capital with two volutes.

**keystone**: The central stone at the top of an arch.

**lights**: Individual window panes, set into a sash, transom or sidelights.

**lintel**: The horizontal beam spanning the top of a window or door.

**louvers**: Fixed or movable slats set into a frame that allow passage of air and light.

**lozenge**: A diamond-shaped ornament applied to a wall surface.

**lunette**: A semicircular window.

**mansard roof**: A roof that is double pitched on all four sides, with a steep lower section and shallow upper section.

**monitor**: A raised portion of a roof, like a cupola, but generally lower and broader.

**monolith**: One solid piece of stone.

**mullion**: Vertical bar or strip, usually made of metal, supporting large panes of glass. *See muntin.*

**muntin**: Bar or strip, usually made of wood, supporting small panes of glass within a sash. *See mullion.*

**neoclassical**: The reuse of classical forms, often in new ways.

**newel post**: An oversized post at the bottom of a stair railing.

**obelisk**: A tall, four-sided shaft that is tapered and crowned with a pyramidal point.

**Palladian window**: A tripartite window with an arched central window and flanking rectangular windows.

**pargeting** (pär'-j□t-□ng): Ornamental plasterwork.

**pavilion**: A projecting element of a façade.

**pediment**: A low, triangular element framed by horizontal and sloping cornices.

**pilaster** (p□-lăs'-tûr): A rectangular, partial column attached to the wall.

**pointed arch**: An arch formed by two equal curves that meet in a point.

**polygonal**: Multi-sided.

**porte-cochère** (pôrt-k□-sh□r'): A covered carriage porch for visitors to disembark from their vehicles.

**portico**: A porch or entry, usually with a pedimented roof supported by classical columns or pilasters.

**proportion**: The relationship of one dimension to another, usually described as a numerical ratio, such as 1:3.

**purlin**: Structural roof member that extends horizontally from gable wall to gable wall.

**pyramidal**: A tapered form with triangular faces that meet in a point.

**quoin** (koin): Unit of stone or brick (or wood resembling those materials) used to accentuate the corners of a building.

**rose window**: An ornamental circular window used in church architecture.

**rustication**: Masonry cut in large blocks separated from each other by deep joints.

**saltbox**: A gable-roof house, with two stories in the front and one in the rear, in which the rear slope extends over the one-story section.

**sash**: A movable frame within a double-hung window in which the panes of a window are set.

**scale**: The size of a building, a component of a building or another element relative to the size of a specific standard, usually the human body.

**segmental arch**: An arch composed of less than half of a circle.

**sidelight**: Narrow windows flanking a doorway.

**skirt**: The lower slope on a mansard roof.

**spire**: A tapering conical or pyramidal element crowning a roof or tower.

**stretcher**: The long side of a brick.

**surround**: The decorative trim on all four sides of a window.

**swag**: An ornamental hanging composed of drapery suspended between two points. *See festoon.*

**swan's neck pediment**: A pediment that is a continuous curve, composed of an S-shaped curve and a reverse S-shaped curve that meet at the top.

**terminate the vista**: Provide a focal point in the middle of a vertically framed view.

**tower**: A prominent vertical structure attached to a church, usually square in plan.

**transom window**: A horizontal window over a door.

**Tudor arch**: A low, wide pointed arch, often with straight legs in the center.

**variety within unity**: Wide variation within a particular form, where the various permutations are consistent and harmonious.

**vault**: An arched ceiling.

**veranda**: A porch.

**vernacular**: Simple in form and ornamentation, in contrast with high style. *See high style.*

**vestibule**: The entrance hall of a church.

**voussoir** (v□-swär'): The wedge-shaped stones composing an arch or vault.

**wet wall**: A masonry wall built with mortar.

# Bibliography

Brownstone, Douglass L. *A Field Guide to America's History.* New York: Facts on File, Inc., 1984.

Ching, Francis D.K. *Architecture: Form, Space & Order*. New York: Van Nostrand Reinhold Company, 1979.

Fleming, John, Hugh Honour and Nikolaus Pevsner. *The Penguin Dictionary of Architecture*. Harmondsworth, England: Penguin Books Ltd., 1972.

Fowler, Martha. "The Shoemaking History of Rochester." *Rochester Times*, May 21, 2009.

Geocities website. http://www.geocities.com/powerofz7/1914.html.

Gottemoeller, Frederick. *Bridgescape: The Art of Designing Bridges.* New York: John Wiley & Sons, Inc., 1998.

Hale, Jonathan. *The Old Way of Seeing.* Boston: Houghton Mifflin Company, 1994.

Klein, Marilyn W., and David P. Fogle. *Clues to American Architecture.* Washington, D.C.: Starhill Press, 1986.

Magnuson, Landis K. "The Last Moving Floor in Action." *Theater Design & Technology* (Fall 2006).

Marlowe, George Francis. *Churches of Old New England*. New York: MacMillan Company, 1947.

McAlester, Virginia, and Lee McAlester. *A Field Guide to American Houses*. New York: Alfred A. Knopf, 1986.

Mouzon, Stephen A. *Traditional Construction Patterns*. New York: McGraw-Hill, 2004.

Nuttgens, Patrick. *Simon and Schuster's Pocket Guide to Architecture*. New York: Simon and Schuster, 1986.

Page, Susan. *The Rochester Opera House*. Brochure. Author, 2008.

Poppeliers, John C., S. Allen Chambers Jr. and Nancy B. Schwartz. *What Style Is It?* Washington, D.C.: Preservation Press, 1983.

Sloane, Eric. *An Age of Barns*. Stillwater, MN: Voyageur Press, Inc., 2001.

Smith, Florence Horne. *Images of America—Rochester*. Dover, NH: Arcadia Publishing, 1996.

Spreiregen, Paul D. *Urban Design: The Architecture of Towns and Cities*. New York: McGraw-Hill, 1965.

Thorson, Robert M. *Exploring Stone Walls*. New York: Walker & Company, 2005.

Turnbull, Craig. *An American Urban Residential Landscape, 1890–1920: Chicago in the Progressive Era*. N.p.: Cambria Press, 2009.

White, Norval. *The Architecture Book*. New York: Alfred A. Knopf, 1976.

Wolfe, Tom. *From Bauhaus to Our House*. New York: Washington Street Press, 1981.

# About the Author

Michael Behrendt is married to Naomi Kornhauser and has two daughters, Liza and Emily. Along with architecture and New Urbanism, he enjoys travel, politics, basketball and juggling. Michael was the 2009 New Hampshire planner of the year, but he is especially proud of having won the 2008 Seacoast Dancing with the Stars competition with his partner, Peggi Morrow. He can be reached at redbaron2@myfairpoint.net or through the publisher.

Visit us at
www.historypress.net